W9-AVH-697

The MOTORBOAT BOOK

BUILD & LAUNCH 20 JET BOATS, PADDLE-WHEELERS, ELECTRIC SUBMARINES & MORE

Ed Sobey

CHICAGO REVIEW PRESS

Central Rappahannock Regional Library
1201 Caroline Street
Fredericksburg, VA 22401

J
623.82
So
c.5

Copyright © 2013 by Ed Sobey
All rights reserved
First edition
Published by Chicago Review Press, Incorporated
814 North Franklin Street
Chicago, Illinois 60610
ISBN 978-1-61374-447-5

Library of Congress Cataloging-in-Publication Data
Sobey, Edwin J. C., 1948–
  The motorboat book : build & launch 20 jet boats, paddle-wheelers, electric submarines & more /
Ed Sobey. — First edition.
     pages cm
Includes bibliographical references.
  ISBN 978-1-61374-447-5
  1. Ship models—Juvenile literature. 2. Motorboats—Juvenile literature. 3. Handicraft—Juvenile
literature. I. Title.
  VM298.S63 2013
  623.82'01044—dc23
                                                                          2012046326

Cover design: Andrew Brozyna, AJB Design, Inc.
Interior design: Rattray Design

Printed in the United States of America
5 4 3 2 1

To Aunt Kay

Contents

3. *Propel That Boat*   29

6. *Projects for a Tiny Sea*   195

Acknowledgments

John Weigant suggested the baking soda model that he remembered from his youth. He related that he spent lots of time in his bathtub as a kid using up his mother's vinegar. John also helped with several experimental models. As always, John, thanks for your ideas.

Professor Alejandro Jenkins at Florida State University provided copies of his research papers on the subject of putt-putt boats. His work is shedding new light on the operation of these enigmatic and fun boats. Thank you, professor.

Thanks too to my wife, Barbara, for her suggestions on several projects and for not complaining about our house being cluttered with models, miscellaneous parts, and failed experiments.

Lastly, thanks go to the kids and teachers who applied their creativity and critical thinking skills to build some of the models shown here.

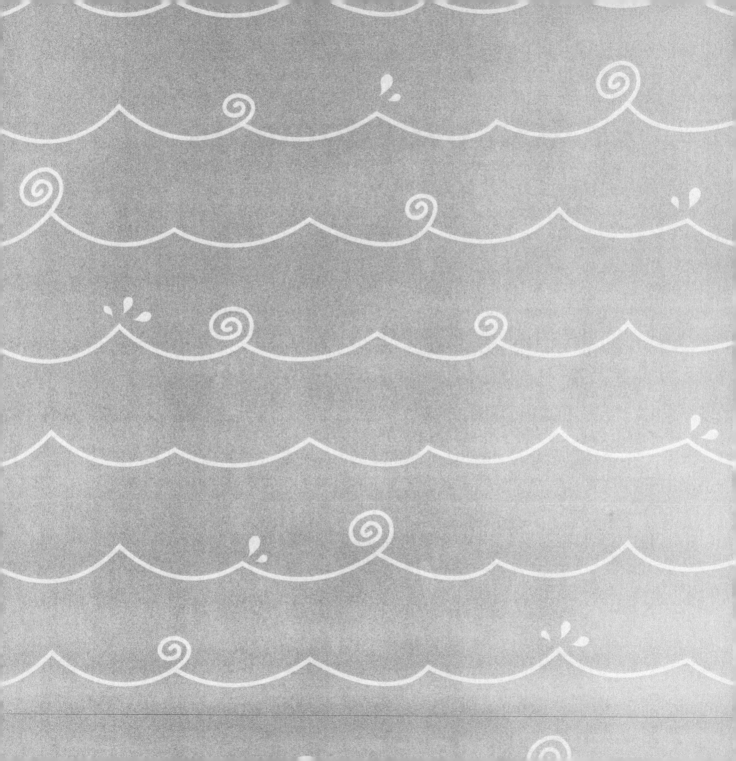

Ahoy!

Messing around with boats is great fun and a wonderful way to learn. By making a model watercraft that really works, you can test your engineering talents and learn patience—and a wide variety of skills.

You will learn science and technology while enjoying the process of building and testing the boats, pumps, and other devices shown in this book. You will also learn the same way that inventors, scientists, and artists learn: by having creative ideas, making models of the ideas, and figuring out how to make the models work. It is the natural way to learn—and the way that best engages people in the process of learning.

If you are a teacher or home school parent, you will find an incredible amount of solid, STEM (science, technology, engineering, and mathematics) content and methods wrapped in the feathers of *The Motorboat Book*. Grab a copy of the STEM standards for your state or country and compare them to the list below. Building these projects leads to understanding of:

- Buoyancy and density
- Chemical reaction
- Design and systems
- Electric circuits
- Energy and energy transformations
- Forces and motion
- Gravity
- Hydraulics
- Investigations and experiments
- Measurement

- Motors
- Nature of matter
- Process of science and engineering investigations

- Solar energy
- Sound
- Use of tools and materials

You have to admit that this is an impressive list of learning topics. It is especially impressive when you consider that anyone making these models will be excited to continue the learning and won't ask, "Is this on the test?" As readers build models, they will develop skills in using tools and materials and will improve their self-confidence. Once skills and understanding have been achieved, people tend to use them. Builders will continue making things using the skills gained and learn new skills along the way.

Appendix B will tell you how to make connections between the science standards and the projects described in this book.

Ship's Log

As founding director of the National Inventors Hall of Fame, I have met many great living inventors. Individually and in groups, they repeatedly expressed the importance of having the opportunity to "mess around" in a shop or laboratory early in their careers. These unstructured experiences gave them the skills and self-confidence to be successful later. Messing around with motorboat projects is a great way to launch children into creative pursuits.

If you are less interested in the learning value and more interested in messing around with boat models, you will still have a blast. I provide the directions but allow you all the latitude you need to build each project your own way. While building you will come up with dozens of new ideas to improve or personalize the models.

That's what I want. My goal is to encourage you to try new technologies, build new designs, and expand on what I suggest. I wish you fair winds and following seas, and many happy hours messing around with *The Motorboat Book*.

1
Start with an Ocean

If you are going to make these models you will need a place to test them and show them off. You need an ocean!

If you have a swimming pool or pond available, you can use either, provided you first give it a suitable name. Since Atlantic, Pacific, and Indian are already taken, come up with a new name for your ocean.

Safety

When you create or use any open body of water, take care that people, especially young children, cannot get into them unsupervised. Even a few inches of water is a hazard for a small child.

If a body aquatic isn't available, build your own. Here are several size options.

Large Oceans

How big would you like to make your ocean? The limitations are the size of level ground you have and the depth of the ocean you need.

For most purposes I find that a good size for an outdoor ocean is 4 feet by 8 feet. Conveniently, hardware stores sell waterproof tarps and sheets of plastic large enough for an ocean of this size. They also carry larger-size materials, or you can duct tape several tarps together if you really need to.

A shallow ocean requires less support and is a safer option than a deeper ocean. As water depth increases, the pressure pushing your ocean apart will increase and require stronger construction. An ocean with a depth of 4 to 6 inches works well, but you may need more water if your models hit bottom.

Adult supervision required

Materials

4 folding tables or similar flat surfaces
Waterproof tarp with grommets, at least 6 feet by 10 feet (larger would be better)
Nylon string
Hose and water supply
3 wooden boards, 1 inch by 8 inches and 8 feet long (optional)
Adult helper (for optional steps)
Saw (optional)
4 hinges with removable pins or other connectors (optional)
Grid wall, 2 feet by 8 feet (optional)
Plastic cable ties (optional)

Build It

1. Any four vertical surfaces that won't move will support your ocean. For a shallow ocean, four folding tables work well. Lay the tables on edge in a square or rectangle, with the legs extended to hold them up.

2. Lay a waterproof tarp over the sides of the tables and secure it with nylon string through its grommets. Then use the hose to fill the tarp with no more than 4 inches of water. This model takes seconds to set up but will support only a shallow ocean. As the number of people using this ocean increases, the number of random bumps increases—think earthquakes and tsunamis—and soon the ocean will fall apart.

3. A more user-friendly model uses wood planks, set on edge, to form the four sea cliffs surrounding the ocean waters. Get three 8-foot-long, 1-inch-by-8-inch boards, and ask an adult to saw one board in half to create two shorter end pieces.

4. There are many ways to hold the boards together. One is to install hinges that have removable pins at the corners where the boards meet. To take down the ocean, remove the pin from the hinge at one of the short ends and let the water swirl out—hopefully into a drain or thirsty grass. Or you can take a trip through a hardware store to find other ideas of how to fasten the boards together. Screws or nails will work if you won't need to take the ocean apart for a while, and a clever builder could devise a system of pegs (nails or dowels) that fit into holes in adjoining boards to hold them in place. Once it's assembled, use the hose to fill your ocean with water—just enough to float your boats.

5. A radically different approach is to use grid wall instead of wood boards. Grid wall is the display rack material used in many retail stores; see appendix A (page 217) for information on where to obtain it. An ideal size for grid wall is 2 feet wide by 8 feet long. The grid wall shown below is 4 feet wide instead, which makes it awkward to put boats into the ocean and retrieve them. The beauty of grid wall is that it sets up in seconds: one person holds two adjoining pieces on edge while another secures them with plastic cable ties. When all four pieces are secured, drape the tarp over the edges and make sure that it lies flat on the ground. Then secure the tarp grommets with more plastic cable ties, and fill the tarp with water. Don't put in more water than you need; as water fills this ocean, it presses outward and will eventually break the cable ties, creating a tsunami. To drain the ocean, cut the cable ties on one of the ends, let the grid wall fall to the ground, and the water will race out.

Science

How many oceans are there? Not counting the one you are building, there are three: the Atlantic, Pacific, and Indian. All three are connected to each other, but the connections are restricted by land masses.

Although the waters mix with each other, each ocean's water has distinctive properties. Some people lump all three oceans into one World Ocean, and other people will separate the three oceans and add the Arctic Ocean or Southern Ocean or both. So you could answer the question of how many oceans exist by saying the earth has one, three, four, or five oceans.

Whatever number you prefer, the water in those oceans covers more than 70 percent of the surface of this planet and makes this planet livable. We should call it Planet Ocean, not Planet Earth.

Smaller Oceans

If you don't need all the space that a large ocean offers, you can test models in plastic storage containers sold at household stores.

Materials

> Plastic storage container at least
>   3 feet long and 6 inches deep
> Bucket
> Water supply

Build It

This photo shows a container that is 3 feet long, 18 inches wide, and 6 inches deep. This type of container is large enough to test that a boat works, but not large enough to see how far or how fast it will go. Clear plastic allows you to peer in from the side to see what is going on underwater. This size is somewhat manageable in that two people can pick up a partially full ocean and carry it slowly to a sink to empty it. It requires only a few buckets of water to fill.

Tiny Seas

For some projects a one- or two-liter bottle provides enough water. See chapter 6 (page 195) for small-sea science projects.

2
Build a Hull

To build a boat, you need a *hull*, the body of your boat. It's what keeps the water out and holds everything else in. It's best to make the hull out of inexpensive and free materials so that any mistakes and do-overs don't break the bank, and you can make lots of boats to try different ideas, technologies, and designs.

Free and Easy Hulls

Collect paper milk and juice containers in the quart and half-gallon size. Using them for motorboats merely interrupts their journey from a refrigerator to the recycling center, and briefly extends their useful life. But one note of caution: if you ask people to save these containers for you, ask them to also rinse them out before setting them aside. The smell of an unwashed milk carton can make a boatbuilder seasick.

Adult supervision required

Materials

Adult helper
Milk or juice cartons made of coated paper
Pocketknife
Scissors

Build It

1. Ask an adult to help you cut the cartons in half, lengthwise. Cutting the ridge at the top of each carton requires a pocketknife, but cutting the rest of the carton can be done with sturdy scissors.

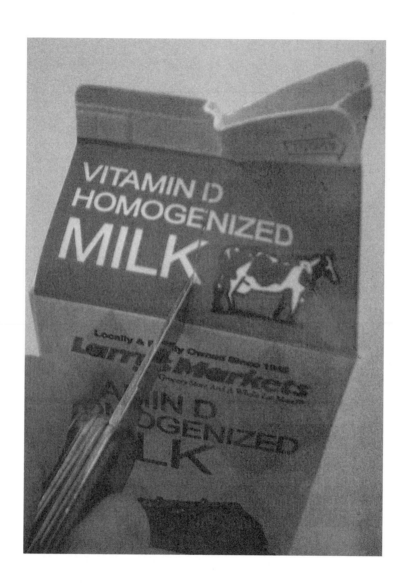

2. The result of lengthwise cutting one carton is two flat-bottom boats that are ready to be propelled. The ridge at the top of the carton becomes the *stem*, or the frontmost part of the boat.

3. Of course, if one hull is good, two hulls are better! Craft sticks and dowels hold the two hulls of this catamaran together. The motor is mounted on the braces between the hulls.

4. To get a V-shaped hull instead of a flat-bottom hull, cut a carton along two opposing edges. These hulls will require *ballast* (something to weigh them down, such as stones) to keep them floating upright.

Ship's Log

In the past, wooden sailing ships carried tons of ballast stones in their *bilges*, or the lowest spaces inside ships. The ballast stones provided stability, especially when a ship was not carrying cargo. One way to identify an old shipwreck on the bottom of the sea is by recognizing the pile of rocks that were used as the ballast.

Modern ships don't use ballast stones, but they do pump water into tanks to weigh down the ship when it is not carrying cargo.

Aluminum Hulls

Aluminum is a great material to use for building hulls. It comes in a variety of thicknesses, is easy to cut, and is strong. Here are two wildly different approaches to using aluminum.

Two-Minute Boats

A fun challenge for anyone is to craft a boat using aluminum foil and test it to see how much weight it will hold before sinking. Galvanized nails, pennies, or metal washers can be the weights. The advantage of having uniform weights is that you count how many pieces you are able to put in your boat before it sinks to compare with the total number of pieces needed to sink other boat designs.

Materials

Aluminum foil
Uniform weights: 1 pound or more of identical small objects
(e.g., nails, washers, or pennies)

Build It

1. Tear off a piece of aluminum foil that is as long as it is wide. Decide if you should make a barge, canoe, or ship. Fold the sides to make your model and give it a test.
2. Add uniform weights to your model one at a time, counting as you add each one. Stop counting when your boat sinks or otherwise touches the bottom of the ocean.
3. For a competition, give everyone the same size piece of foil and no other materials. Each player should bend, fold, and shape the aluminum foil to make a boat. Once all the boats are finished, players should place them in water and start loading them with the uniform weights, counting as they go. Everyone will want

a second chance and a new piece of foil to test their new ideas on what makes an ideal shape.

Science

Why does a boat sink? Most boats and ships are made of materials that, if compressed into a ball, would sink quickly. The materials a ship is made of are heavier than an equal volume of water. But the ship or boat floats because it is a hole in the ocean filled with air, where the sides of the hole are the ship's hull. The hull keeps water out.

If you replace the air inside the hole with water, which is about a thousand times denser than air, the ship sinks. Since the heavy materials in the ship weigh more per volume than water and there is nothing light inside to buoy the ship up, down she goes. At sea, this is a bad day.

Extruded Aluminum Boat Hulls

A sturdier hull can be made from a disposable aluminum roasting pan. This isn't quick and easy, but it is fun and turns out very nice boat hulls. These hulls are best used with small electric motors or steam putt-putt engines.

The process is to cut a mold out of wood and to squeeze (or *extrude*) the aluminum into the mold. Once you make the mold, you can create as many identical boats as you want.

Adult supervision required

Materials

Adult helper
Wooden board, 1 inch by 4 inches and at least 2 feet long
Wood saw
Coping saw
Pencil
Cereal box (empty)
Ruler
Scissors
Large C-clamp
Workbench
Wood glue
4 small C-clamps
Aluminum roasting pan (disposable)

Build It

1. Ask an adult to cut a 6-inch length of a 1-inch-by-4-inch board using a wood saw. Your boat's hull will be smaller than these dimensions, so you will end up with a form (the size and shape of your finished boat) and mold (a cavity) you can push the form into.

2. Draw the shape of the hull that you want on the inside of an empty cereal box, and then draw a straight line through that shape, from the stem to the middle of the *stern*, the back end of the boat. Cut out the hull shape, then cut along the center line as well so you have two half-hull shapes. From these two pieces of cardboard, pick the one you like best; you'll use it to draw the full hull shape on the wood.

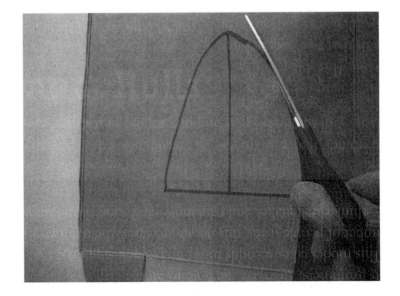

3. Measure the center of the two short sides of the wood your adult helper cut so you can draw a center line. Align the cereal box shape along the center line, making sure that you are leaving enough wood (more than ¼ inch) all the way around the shape so the mold won't break. Trace the outer edge of the cardboard form. Flip the cardboard over and trace it (now upside down) on the other side.

4. Clamp the wood firmly to a workbench and ask your adult helper to cut out the shape with the coping saw. This inexpensive saw allows the user to turn corners easily. Your helper should keep the blade vertical while he or she cuts, starting from the outer edge of the wood and sawing into the hull shape you have drawn, following the line all the way around. To make the cutting easier at the far end, he or she can cut the mold through to the end of the block of wood. It doesn't matter if the mold ends up in two parts. When your helper has cut around the shape you

have drawn, you will have a piece of wood in the shape you designed—the *plug* (or form) and a *mold* that has either one or two pieces.

5. Lay the one or two pieces of the mold on top of another 6-inch-long piece of the 1-inch-by-4-inch board. Glue the mold to the new piece of wood. Use wood glue and four small C-clamps to hold it while it dries.

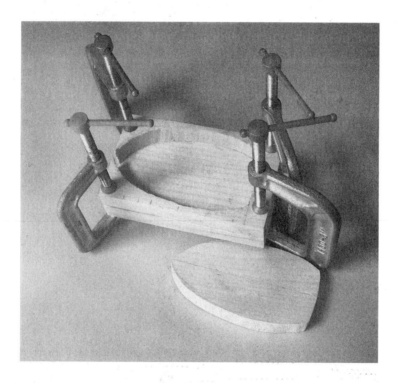

6. While the glue is drying, use scissors to cut a piece of aluminum from a disposable roasting pan. The piece must to be larger than the plug since you need additional material to form the sides of the boat, not just the bottom.

7. After the glue has dried, place the piece of aluminum on top of the mold. Put the plug on top of the aluminum so it is aligned with the shape of the mold and can fit into it. Use a large C-clamp to force the plug into the mold. If the plug isn't

going in evenly, release the clamp and reposition it to the high spot—where the wood sticks up the highest—and then clamp down again.

8. When the clamp has pushed the plug down evenly into the mold, unscrew the clamp and remove the hull. Trim the hull with scissors, but to eliminate sharp

edges, leave some excess material as you trim. Then fold this excess inside the boat to leave a folded edge around the top of the hull.

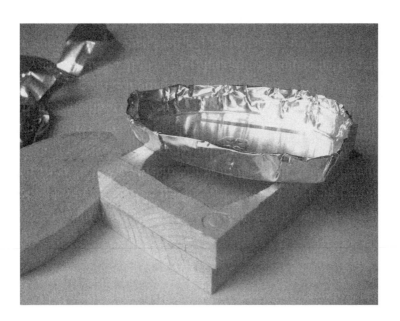

Other Hull Materials

Many other materials make good boat hulls. You can use styrene meat trays, which you can purchase in bulk at restaurant supply stores. If you only need a few, a friendly butcher at the grocery store will likely give them to you, or you can wash and recycle trays that your family might have left over from a meal.

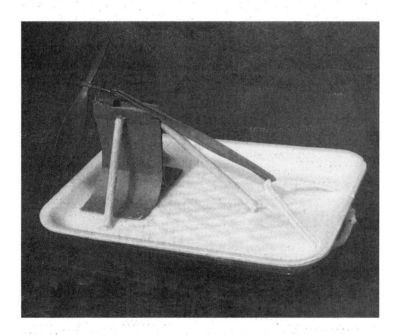

Meat trays are easy to cut with scissors and float well. On the negative side, they don't have much *free board* (height from the water level to the top of the edge of the boat), they aren't easy to attach things to, and the styrene doesn't have much strength or ability to bend. For many projects, you will use a hot glue gun, and this will melt the styrene, making it more difficult to hold pieces together.

Styrene and coated paper plates work for some models. The model shown below is a gravity boat, and the large symmetrical surface of a disposable plate works especially well as it spreads the weight evenly. The symmetrical shape, however, is difficult to steer and is slow moving through the water.

Other materials also work. Rubber ducks are fun but are difficult to cut and more expensive. For most "messing around" projects, less expensive materials are more desirable.

Science

Ship and boat hulls are made of a wide variety of materials. We think most often of boats made of wood and ships of steel. But fiberglass, aluminum, and plastic are also used in boats, and concrete and ferro-cement are used in ships.

What's the Difference?

A *boat* is a small vessel, while a *ship* is much larger. That distinction isn't always that clear, so sailors put it a different way: a boat is a vessel that's small enough to be carried on a ship.

3
Propel That Boat

How many ways can you think of to propel your boat across the ocean? Lots! As you build these models you'll think of variations to these designs or even brand-new ones. That's part of the fun of messing around with boats.

Sails

When people think of making a sailboat, most picture square sails rather than the fore and aft sails more commonly used today. (*Fore* means that something is toward the forward, or front, part of a ship or boat, while *aft* means it's toward the after, or back, part.) Scraps of fabric work well for fore and aft sails. For square sails, plastic bags or even sheets of paper will do.

Adult supervision required

Materials

Milk carton hull (page 10) plus
   additional pieces of milk carton
Scissors
Dowel, 6 inches long, ¼-inch diameter

Hot glue gun
String (optional)
Plastic bag, paper, index cards, or cloth
Battery-powered fan

Build It

1. Start with the quick and easy hull cut out of a paper milk or juice carton.
2. Attach a dowel mast to the hull. The biggest challenge is how to hold a mast upright. Simply gluing the bottom of the mast to the hull won't provide enough strength to withstand a breeze, let alone a gale. However, you can stabilize the mast by either tying strings (sailors call these *stays* and *shrouds* depending on where they attach to the boat) or using pieces cut from a milk carton. The first way is difficult and requires nimble fingers and patience. Bracing the mast with a piece of milk carton that is glued to the side of the hull is fast and easy.
3. A plastic bag, as shown at the top of the next page, is an obvious material for sails. So is paper or an index card.

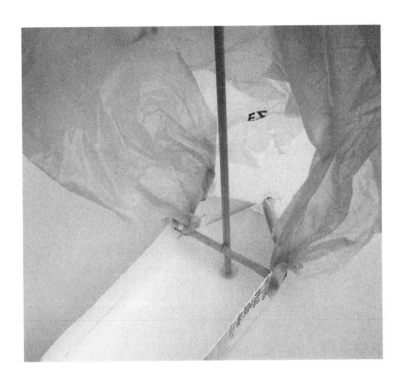

Safety

To drive your sailboat *do not* use an electric fan powered through a wall socket. *Keep all electrical appliances away from the wet testing areas.*

Test It

To move a sailboat you could either wait for a strong wind or push the sail with a battery-powered fan. Discount stores sell these fans for a couple of dollars. Hold the fan in your hand and have it blow onto the sail.

How would it work if you mounted the fan to the boat? If you're not sure, do this experiment. First blow on the sail with a handheld fan to see how fast the boat moves, then repeat the experiment by temporarily taping the fan to the inside of the hull of the boat. Mounted in the boat, the fan will be pushing itself (and the boat) in one direction and pushing the sail in the opposite direction, so the boat won't move.

Sailing Further

I once saw a creative student make a sailboat in less than two minutes. He cut two slits in the top edge of a styrene cup and used the slits to hold a piece of paper. To keep the cup upright in the water, he dropped in three or four stones. Done!

Gravity-Powered Boat

Building a gravity-powered model car sounds reasonable. Put a model on an inclined ramp and let it go. How about a gravity-powered model *boat*? If you hold the water surface at an inclined angle the boat will move, but so will all the water. So how can you use gravity to propel a boat?

Instead of tipping the surface of the water to propel the boat, pile up the water inside the boat and let it flow out. Make a water jet where gravity supplies the force to squirt the water out the stern of the boat.

Adult supervision required

Materials

Disposable plate (paper, plastic, or styrene)
Hot glue gun
Disposable cup (paper or styrene)
Scissors
Pocketknife with awl, or a sharp pencil
Drinking straws, regular and milkshake/fat size
Small container to refill the cup

Build It

1. The ideal hull for this boat is a disposable plate made of either coated paper, plastic, or styrene. Paper is preferable: it's easier to glue to and doesn't break or tear when you cut it.

2. Hot glue a disposable styrene or paper cup onto the center of the plate, with the open end up.

3. Make a small hole in the side of the cup for a straw to fit through. A pencil can poke through the cup as will the awl on a pocketknife. See the picture below for placement.

4. Slide a straw through the hole. The straw should extend across the edge of the plate so that it will release water overboard and not into your hull. You may need to seal the hole in the cup around the straw with a dribble of hot glue.

Test It

You are now ready to test your boat. Use a small container to scoop up some water from your ocean and pour it into the cup on the boat. Then put the boat on the water surface. As water drains out of the cup in one direction, the boat will move in the opposite direction.

Sailing Further

Here is where you can be creative. How can you get the gravity boat to move even faster? You could add another straw or a straw with a larger diameter—a fat straw or milkshake straw. How large a straw or tube could you use?

If you use multiple straws, in what direction do the straws have to point so the boat moves faster? Your experiments will answer these questions and demonstrate the laws of motion.

Gravity-Powered Boat with Electric Pump

Do you like the Gravity-Powered Boat, but want it to travel farther? Instead of pouring water into the cup, pump it in. Use a small, battery-powered pump to lift water into the cup so it can flow out through the straw.

Adult supervision required

Materials

Milk carton hull (page 10)
Pocketknife with awl
Disposable cup
Drinking straw, milkshake/fat size
Drill bit (the same diameter as the straw)
Hot glue gun
Battery-operated pump
9-volt battery, or 2 or 4 AA batteries
    in battery pack
Paper clip
2 alligator clip leads
Vinyl tubing to fit the pump discharge

Build It

1. Switch from a styrene plate hull to a milk carton hull to make it easier to attach the pump.
2. With an awl, make a small hole in the base of a disposable cup. This model uses a paper cup. Use a drill bit to enlarge the hole so a milkshake straw will just barely fit through. This larger straw will drive the boat faster and will keep up with the pump so the cup doesn't overflow. Note how short the straw is in the photo. Water flowing through a straw loses energy by rubbing on the sides of the straw and comes out the end moving slower. The shorter the straw is, the faster the water moves and the faster the boat moves. Slide the straw into the hole and seal the hole with hot glue.

3. Use an awl to make a hole just above the deck in the *transom*, the back panel of the milk carton hull. Hand twist a drill bit to enlarge the hole so the milkshake straw fits through. Place the cup with straw in the boat and slide the straw through the hole in the transom. Seal the straw in place with hot glue and glue the cup to the deck.

4. Mount the pump. The pump shown below draws water up from the bottom and pushes it out through a circular opening at the top of the pump. I could have attached the pump to the outside of the hull, but that would have been awkward with the motor hanging overboard. Instead, I cut out a section of the hull (allowing water to enter the intake hole) and mounted the pump there, using hot glue to seal the seam between the hull and pump. This keeps the boat from sinking. Check the geometry of the pump you get to see where best to locate it.

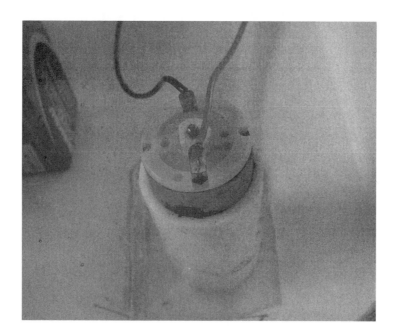

5. Secure the discharge hose. I inserted a ¼-inch vinyl tube into the discharge port and took the other end to the cup. To hold it in position in the cup, make a hole in the side of the cup with the awl and slide the tube through it.

6. Put a dab of hot glue on the side of a 9-volt battery to hold it to the side of the boat. Use two alligator clip leads to make the electrical connections between the battery and the pump. Pinching the leads to open them, attach one end of each clip lead to the wires or terminals (small metals tabs) on the pump, and the other ends of the clip leads to the battery's positive and negative terminals.

Test It

With the connections made, the pump pushed water into the cup, and after a few seconds, the boat started moving. Nine volts was probably more voltage than this pump needed, so I could have replaced it with a battery pack of two or four AA batteries.

If the straw empties the cup faster than the pump can fill the cup (or "build up head"), place a paper clip across the end of the straw to reduce the rate of discharge. If the cup fills faster than the water discharges through the straw or tube, add a second straw.

Balloon-Powered Boat

The basic idea here is simple: inflate a balloon attached to a boat and let it deflate to push the boat. Getting it to work well allows you to exercise your creative engineering skills. The goal is to get your boat to go as far as possible in one direction.

Adult supervision required

Materials

Drinking straws, regular and milkshake/fat size
Latex balloons, 12-inch diameter
Masking tape
Vinyl tubing, variety of sizes (optional)
Pocketknife with awl
Milk carton hull (page 10)
Scissors
Paper clip (optional)

Build It

1. Insert a straw into the mouth of a 12-inch-diameter latex balloon and wrap the excess latex of the mouth around the straw so you can tape it and seal it. You want the balloon wrapped around the straw so that the air can enter or leave the balloon only through the straw. You need only an inch or two of tape, but you do need the latex to wrap smoothly and tightly around the straw. The width of the drinking

straw will determine how far the boat can go; a straw that's too narrow will make it difficult to inflate the balloon. A standard-size drinking straw and a milkshake or fat straw are a good start. To experiment further, get a variety of sizes of vinyl tubing from a hardware store to use instead of the straws. Purchase 1 foot of each size up to ½ inch.

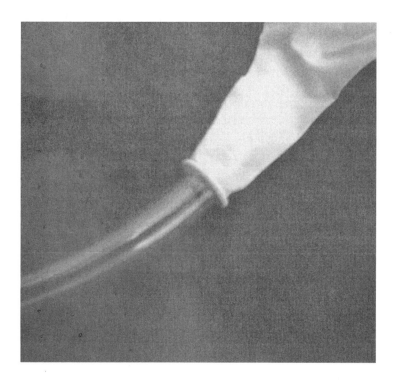

2. Where do you want the air from the balloon to come out? Should it vent into the air or into the water? Does it matter? Use an awl to poke a hole through the transom of a milk carton hull so the straw can slide through and vent into the air

or water. If the air is coming out of the back of the boat, what direction will the boat move?

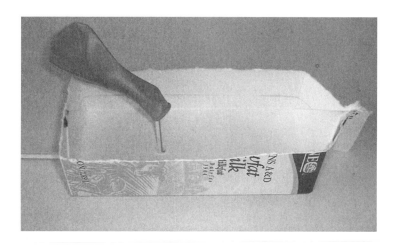

Test It

Inflate the balloon by blowing through the straw. Pinch the neck of the balloon above the straw to keep air in the balloon between breaths and after filling the balloon.

When the balloon is inflated, slide the straw through the hole in the transom. Use a piece of masking tape to hold the balloon in position on top of the hull. A spare pair of hands will make this easier. Then let go of the balloon.

Did the boat move? If it didn't, one of three things is happening. First, air could be leaking out between the mouth of the balloon and the straw. Second, the straw could be too large, which allows the air to rush out in a "whoosh," without pushing the boat. Or third, the straw could be too small, which restricts the air so much it doesn't provide enough force to move the boat. You can speed up and slow down the rate of deflation by changing the width of the straws or by cutting them shorter. The shorter a straw is, the less drag it exerts on the exhausting air and the faster the air comes out.

Does the boat move in a straight line? Adjust the angle of the straw to adjust the direction of travel. If your boat turns left, angle the straw to the right. This will push the stern to the left, which will bring the *bow*, the front of the boat, around to the right.

Sailing Further

Listen to your boat. Does it make the putt-putt sound of an old outboard motor? To get a great putt-putt sound, make sure the end of the straw vents underwater so the air comes out into the water. If you don't hear the engine sound with the straw in the water, slide a paper clip across the straw. Then it should make a sound.

Will two balloons push a boat twice as far? Often a two-balloon boat doesn't travel as far because it is hard to get the two balloons to push the boat forward without interfering with each other. You can get it to work, but it isn't as easy as it first appears. An enterprising student of mine inserted one balloon inside another balloon and used that double balloon to propel his boat. Blowing up the double balloon was his biggest problem, but the boat went far.

Here's another topic to explore. If you watch closely you will see the boat accelerate forward just moments before the balloon has emptied. The boat was traveling at a constant speed and then speeded up before coasting to a stop. Why did it accelerate at the end?

You already know the answer, but possibly haven't connected your knowledge with this observation. When you blow up a balloon, the first and second breaths are the hardest. After that, it's easier to inflate. The balloon exerts the greatest pressure when it is small, due to its geometry. As the balloon deflates it gets to a point where the pressure is greater than it had been, and the increased airflow causes the boat to accelerate.

Ship's Log

Sir Michael Faraday was the first person to make latex or rubber balloons. He needed a way to collect gases for his experiments on fermentation, so he cut circles out of latex and pressed the edges together. Someone else saw the opportunity in making balloons, and within a year of Faraday's first balloon they were selling balloons as toys.

Science

Try this experiment. Collect two pull-up nozzles from plastic water bottles. Use hot glue to stick their bases together, making sure there is a good seal all the way around the perimeters of the lids. Attach identical balloons to each nozzle, with one balloon inflated with just a few puffs of air and the other one inflated nearly full. Keep the valves (pull-up nozzles) closed while you think about this question: What will happen when you pull open the nozzles and let air flow between the two balloons?

Nearly everyone says that the "balloons will even out." They are both right and wrong. The pressure inside the two balloons will equilibrate or even out, but the balloons' size will not. The balloon that is larger will get larger still. The smaller balloon will get smaller.

With the valves open, squeeze the smaller balloon to force air into the larger balloon. When you release your grip, air will flow back into the smaller balloon. The air inside the two balloons is the same—it's at the same pressure.

Rubber Band–Powered Boats

Rubber bands store energy that is released as they return to their original size from a stretch. There are many ways to use the stored energy of a stretched rubber band to propel a boat. Three different boat models follow.

Nose Hook Boat

Nose hooks are mechanisms that power rubber band airplanes. A plastic piece fits onto the balsa frame of the airplane. It holds the propeller and a loop of wire to hold one end of a rubber band. You wind up the propeller to twist the rubber band and store energy in it. On releasing the propeller, it spins in the opposite direction as the rubber band unwinds. You can collect nose hooks from rubber band–powered balsa planes or buy them in bulk from science supply stores.

Adult supervision required

Materials

Dowel, 10 inches long, ¼-inch diameter
Pocketknife or sanding block
Nose hook and propeller
Hot glue gun
Rubber bands
Styrene meat tray hull (page 24) or milk carton hull (page 10)
Plastic cup or other material for motor mount
Paper clip or nail (optional)

Build It

1. Make the motor. You can use a dowel to separate the propeller and the other end of the rubber band. Shave or sand one end of a 10-inch-long dowel so it will fit into the plastic cap on the nose hook. Drop two dabs of hot glue into the plastic cup and insert one end of the dowel. When the glue has dried, stretch a rubber band from the loop of wire on the nose hook to the far end of the dowel.

2. Hot glue the rubber band motor to the hull. The model shown below uses an empty yogurt cup as a motor mount. It raises the motor high enough so the propeller doesn't hit the boat. This design works well.

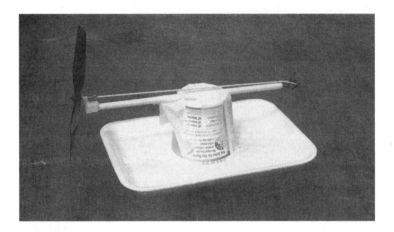

3. Here is the same concept using a milk carton hull. The propeller is angled upward and wastes some of its energy trying to lift the boat off the water (or push it down, depending on how it turns), but otherwise it works well.

Sailing Further

How about using the nose hook to push water rather than air? In the boat below, the nose hook was mounted directly onto the styrene meat tray hull with the rubber band anchored into the hull with a nail or paper clip. A slot was cut in the hull so the propeller could push water rather than air.

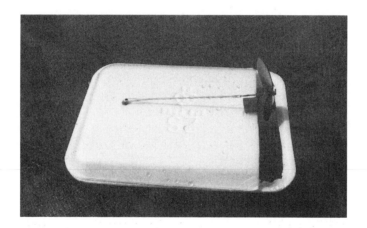

The viscosity (or stickiness) and density of water are so much higher than for air that they dramatically slow down the propeller's rate of spin. Rather than propelling the boat forward, the now slowly turning propeller pushes the boat to one side.

Stern Wheeler or Paddle-Wheeler

This is the design of the old riverboats that traveled up and down the Mississippi River. A large paddle with a number of blades rotates to push the ship forward.

Materials

Milk carton hull (page 10) plus additional pieces of milk carton
2 craft sticks or similarly sized dowels
Duct tape
Scissors
2 dowels, 4 inches long, ⅛-inch diameter (optional)
Hot glue gun (optional)
Rubber band

Build It

1. Use a milk carton hull for this boat. Mount a craft stick or dowel on each side of the stern of the boat. The wood should extend at least 3 inches behind the boat. Because the rubber band will pull the ends of the craft sticks or dowels together, it will pull the other end away from the boat hull. To hold the sticks solidly against the side of the boat, wrap duct tape around them and the boat hull.

2. To make the paddle, cut two rectangles out of a paper milk carton. Each rectangle can be 3 inches by 4 inches. Cut a narrow slot into the middle of the longer side (the 4-inch side) of each paddle, halfway across the paddle. Then align the slots on the two paddles and insert one into the other.

3. Add a small piece of duct tape into the edges where the two paddle blades meet. This taping or gluing should hold the two blades 90 degrees apart.

4. ***With adult supervision***, you can make an even stronger paddle, by reinforcing it with two 4-inch-long pieces of ⅛-inch dowel. On the paddle, add a bead of hot glue to one of the points where the two blades meet and push one dowel into the molten glue. ***Be careful not to burn your fingers.*** Glue the second piece of dowel to the intersection on the opposite side of the paddle.

5. Finally, whichever version of the paddle you decide to use, it's time to attach it to the boat. Stretch a rubber band between the two protruding ends of the dowels or craft sticks. Slide the paddle between the two leaves of the rubber band. You're ready to go.

Test It

Wind up the paddle more times than you think are necessary and release the boat in water. Which way did the boat move? To get the boat moving *forward* (in the direction of the pointy end of the boat), the paddle has to push water *backward*. To get the paddle to push backward, twist the paddle in the opposite direction.

Sailing Further

If a stern paddle pushes the boat well, consider adding a bow paddle! Follow the same building directions, but mount the dowels or craft sticks off the bow (front) of the boat so the paddle can pull it forward. With help from a friend, you can operate both bow and stern paddles at the same time.

Science

If you didn't know the laws of motion before, you certainly are learning them now. To get the boat moving forward, you have to push air (balloon boats) or water (paddleboats) in the opposite direction.

Side Wheeler or Side Paddle-Wheeler

The earliest steamboats had large paddles mounted *amidships*—at the center of the boat—on each side. You can make a rubber band model using the same idea.

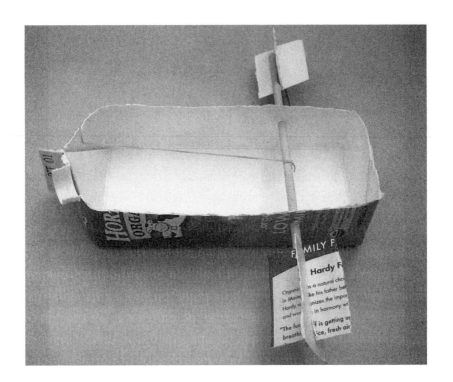

Materials

Milk carton hull (page 10)
Single hole punch
Dowel, 10 inches long, ¼-inch diameter
Scissors
Hot glue gun
Rubber bands
Paper clip

Build It

1. Use a milk carton hull for this project. Use the hole punch to make a hole in each side of the boat at the same location, in the middle of the boat or near the stern. The middle boat position looks more authentic, but the stern position for the paddle allows you to use a longer rubber band, and therefore get more distance in each voyage. One of the challenges with this design is reducing the loss of energy due to friction as the axle rubs against the edges of each hole. Using a hole punch will make clean holes and reduce friction. Position the holes low enough so the paddles will touch the water.

2. Make two sets of paddles following the instructions for the Stern Wheeler (page 51). Slide a 10-inch-long dowel through the two holes.

3. To mount the paddles onto the axle (dowel), dribble hot glue along one seam of a paddle, where the two blades meet. Press this against the end of the axle and hold

it until the hot glue dries. ***Be careful not to burn your fingers.*** Repeat on the other side for the second paddle.

4. Cut a rubber band to get one long elastic strand. Tie one end to a paper clip. Cut a slot near the bow of the boat and slide the rubber band into the slot. The paper clip now serves as a toggle, preventing the rubber band from slipping out. Wrap the other end of the rubber band around the axle and wind the axle up so each new wrapping lies on top of the previous wrapping.

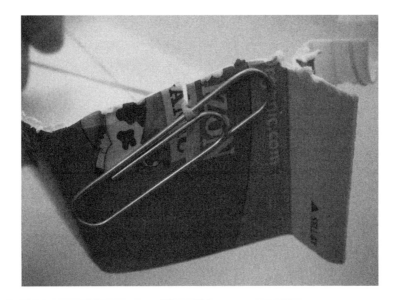

Sailing Further

The most common problem with making a side wheeler is that the paddles don't touch the water. Make sure that when you punch the holes they are low enough, or that your paddle blades are big enough so the bottoms of each blade are able to grab water.

Another problem: if the rubber band slides off the axle, try hot gluing it and then, after the glue dries, winding the band up on top of the spot where you glued it.

Electric Boats

These are my favorite boats. There are many creative ways to use the motion of a small electric motor to move a boat. Here are some designs to start. After you make each one, rip it apart and build another one or try your own variation of the design shown here.

"Electric boats?" you might say. "But electricity is dangerous!" Yes, 110-volt alternating current, the stuff that you find in a wall socket, is dangerous near water. But you'll be using batteries that at most have 9 volts and relatively low power.

To see for yourself, try this experiment. Touch the two terminals of a 9-volt battery to your tongue. This won't be a fun experience, but it won't hurt. You will feel a slightly unpleasant tingling in your tongue. Next, wipe off the battery and hold the two terminals against your arm. You won't feel a thing. Moisten your arm and try it again. Wet skin conducts electricity much better than dry skin does, but unless you lick the battery, you won't feel anything.

To power these models use only 9-volt "transistor" batteries or any of the cylindrical batteries that deliver 1.5 volts. These are AAA, AA, C, and D cells.

Swamp Boat

Have you seen the flat-bottom boats that fly through the Everglades? Maybe you've ridden on one. There is a big propeller at the back of the boat that pushes air to the rear to make the boat go forward. The Swamp Boat here is a version of this airboat.

This boat is quick to build and works well. It allows lots of creativity in improving the basic design. An inexpensive toy motor spins a propeller that pushes air to move the boat. The motor is powered by a 9-volt battery.

Adult supervision required

Materials

Milk carton hull (page 10) or
    styrene meat tray hull (page 24)
Plastic cup or other material for motor mount
Toy motor
Hot glue gun
Three-bladed propeller
Adult helper
9-volt battery
2 alligator clip leads
Switch (optional)
Scissors

Build It

1. Start with a milk carton hull. (Later you will see a model using a styrene meat tray that also works well.)
2. You will need to raise the motor and propeller above the hull so that the blades can spin freely in the air. Look around for a disposable cup or yogurt container on which you will mount the motor. In this model, the motor was taped to a plastic cup that was glued to the milk carton. Masking tape doesn't last long in water; use hot glue instead. Put a generous dab on one side of the motor, making sure you don't get any into the cooling ports. Press the motor against the cup or whatever you are using as a motor stand. The glue holds, but not so strongly that you can't pull off the motor later. Have an adult help you push the three-bladed propeller onto the motor shaft. Make sure that it's on as far as it can go.

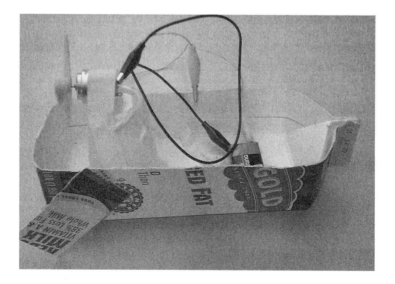

3. Glue the cup to the bottom of the boat, making sure it is amidships so it won't tip the boat over. Use just a dribble of glue because you will want to reposition the cup after you see how well the boat works. Even with the motor facing directly aft, it will not push the boat straight ahead, so you will want to rotate the cup to counteract the boat's tendency to turn.

4. The 9-volt battery has about the same weight as the motor, so you need to place it near the bow to balance the boat fore and aft. Hold it in place with a small dab of hot glue.

Test It

Before launching your boat, test the motor. Use two alligator clip leads to connect the motor to the battery. The motor has two small metal tabs on the end opposite the motor shaft; attach a different clip lead to each tab. Connect the other ends of the clip leads to the positive and negative terminals on the battery; marks on the sides of the battery should indicate which is which. Which way will the propeller spin? Will it turn clockwise or counterclockwise? Watch the propeller and remember which direction it moves.

The propeller should spin very fast. It will spin so fast that it makes a humming sound. So fast that *if you stick a finger into the blade it will hurt!* Keeping your fingers out of the path of the blades, feel which direction the air is being pushed. Is that the direction you want the air to go? If not, reverse the leads to the battery. That is, put the lead that is on the positive battery terminal on the negative terminal, and the lead that is on the negative battery terminal on the positive terminal. Switching the two connections at one end (either the battery end or the motor end, but not both) will change the direction of the flow of electrons through the circuit and the direction that the motor spins. After you switch the wires, test the direction again; it should be reversed.

The boat should move smartly across your ocean. However, it probably won't be going in a straight line. It will consistently turn to one side or the other.

Sailing Further

To solve the problem of turning, you can do several things. One is to reposition the motor so that it does not blow straight backward but to one side, to counteract the boat's tendency to turn. Another solution is to add *skegs*, the fins shown at the bottom left of the photo on page 62, to keep the boat going in a straight line. On a sailboat, these would be called *leeboards*, while a *keel* would be a single stabilizing structure along the center of the hull.

The model below shows some variations on the same theme. This boat's designer added a fixed rudder to help keep the boat going straight. The rudder needed to be larger to be more effective. The motor mount was built from pieces of ⅛-inch balsa wood strips cut to a 1-inch width. The balsa was hot glued together. The designer also added a switch to the circuit. This knife blade switch allows the captain to control the motor (on and off) without messing around with the clip leads.

In the third model below, the designer built a raised platform out of styrene to hold two motors. Both motors are powered by one battery, which results in both motors turning much more slowly than with one motor per battery. But the boat moved well. By adjusting the position of the motors on the mount, the direction of the boat could be changed.

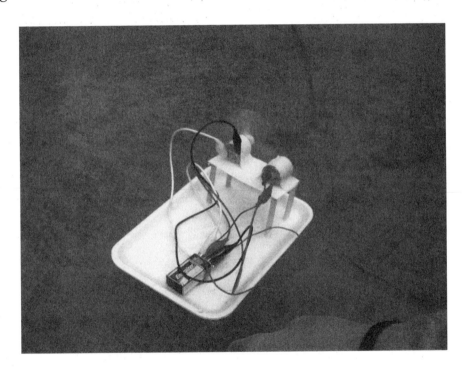

Ship's Chandlery

When buying propellers, pulleys, and gears, always check the size of the center hole. Make sure it is the same size as the diameter of the shaft of the motor you are buying. If it's not, you will need to make adjustments. If the motor shaft is larger, you can drill out the hole in the plastic propeller or other components with a hand or electric drill.

If the hole in the propeller is larger than the shaft, you have several options. If they are nearly the same size, wrap a tiny piece of tape around the motor shaft. Force the propeller onto the wrapped shaft. If the hole and the shaft are vastly different in size, you can insert a dowel that fits the hole and glue it in place. Then drill a hole in the dowel that will just fit the motor shaft. Glue it in place on the motor shaft.

None of these options, however, will get the propeller mounted exactly in line with the motor shaft and the propeller will wobble, especially at high speeds. Check out appendix A (page 217) for suggestions on where to purchase propellers, pulleys, and gears.

Even Easier Swamp Boat

Not only is this design easier and quicker to build—it takes about one minute—but it is also less expensive.

Adult supervision required

Materials

Battery-powered fan   Milk carton hull (page 10)
Hot glue gun

Build It

1. Get a cheap, battery-powered fan. Discount stores sell these for a dollar or two at most, and that cost includes a battery!
2. Glue the fan to the bottom of the milk carton hull with a dab of hot glue. Later you can rip the fan off the boat with no harm to the fan or boat.

3. Go test your boat.

Motor Duck DUKW

A DUKW, pronounced "duck," is an amphibious vehicle, meaning it can be driven both in the water and on land. Designed to move people and cargo between sea and shore during World War II, DUKWs disappeared from view until recently, when a new use was discovered for them: giving tourists unique tours of cities on lakes and bays.

The challenge in this project is to make a vehicle that rolls across the ground and into a body of water, and continues across the water. A swimming pool is ideal for this. You might need to build a ramp to let your DUKW drive into your pool or other test ocean.

You don't have to use a rubber duck, as you will see here, but why not? To get a motor and battery inside a rubber duck, the duck must be 5 inches long or larger.

Materials

Large rubber duck (5 inches long or larger)
Sharp pocket knife
Adult helper
Toy motor
Acorn clips (optional)
2 or 3 alligator clip leads
9-volt battery
Paper clip (optional)
Propeller
Wheels
Dowels to fit the wheels (in this model they are ⅛-inch diameter)
Drinking straws, regular and milkshake
Duct tape (what else?)
Hot glue gun (optional)
Film canisters (35 mm; optional)
2 styrene meat trays (optional)
Small cardboard box (optional)
Milk carton hull (optional; page 10)

Build It

1. Rubber duck skin is tough to cut, even with a sharp pocketknife, so ask an adult for help. Decide where to place the motor and cut as small an opening as you can to get it in place. The model on the next page has a tail opening holding the motor

and a top flap to change the battery. The designer cleverly added two brass acorn clips to the side of the duck. A clip lead connects the battery (inside) to the motor. Another alligator clip lead connects the other battery terminal to one of the acorn clips. A third alligator clip lead connects the other motor terminal to the second acorn clip. To power the motor, the designer closes the circuit by rotating the large paper clip so it touches both acorn clips. (The wheels haven't yet been added to this model.) The propeller is pushed onto the motor shaft.

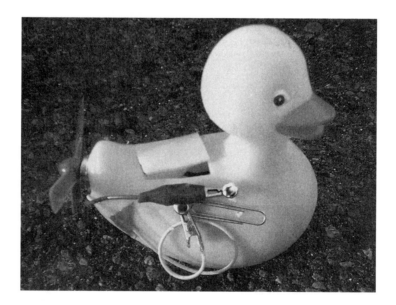

2. Add axles and wheels to your DUKW. Two dowels serve as axles in the model on the next page. The axles run through short sections of a drinking straw that are taped to the bottom of the duck. Push the wheels onto the ends of the dowels. The tape didn't last long in the water, but the duck did manage to drive across a land

bridge and into the pond. (Instead of duct tape, you could also try using hot glue.) The bigger issue with this duck was that all the weight was mounted on its back, high above the center of buoyancy and balance. It was more stable upside down than right side up, and quickly flipped over.

3. The three-wheel Motor Duck DUKW below shows several modifications to keep it upright. Film canisters were added to the sides for additional *buoyancy*—to help the DUKW float. The battery was mounted far to the rear to keep the duck from tipping forward under the weight of the motor that is mounted in the chest of the duck. The structure that holds the axles is made of milkshake straws.

4. The vehicle at the top of the next page is a Motor Duck DUKW in name only. Two styrene meat trays are taped together to form the hull. Milkshake straws pass through the bottom tray to hold the axles. The duck body has disappeared and all that can be seen is its head. The motor is mounted on top of a small cardboard box to raise it high enough so the propeller doesn't hit the water.

Sailing Further

If you find yourself duck-less, you can still build a DUKW. Below is a DUKW without a duck. Straws have been hot glued to the underside of the milk carton hull to serve as bearings for the axles that hold the wheels. The DUKW rolls across a dry surface and floats across the ocean powered by the propeller.

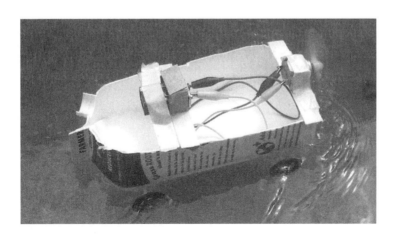

Ship's Log

Someone at General Motors must have spent a long time thinking up the name DUKW for the amphibious vehicles. *D* designates that the vehicle was designed in 1942, and *U* means it is a utility vehicle. A utility vehicle is one able to travel over rough ground. The *K* means that it has front-wheel drive, and the *W* means that the two rear axles are also powered. All six wheels drive the DUKW.

Science

The chemical reaction in any type of battery provides the same voltage regardless of the size of battery cell. One AA battery provides 1.5 volts, as does a C cell, D cell, and AAA. However, the larger the battery is, the longer it will deliver that voltage.

To make a 9-volt battery, manufacturers pack six cells together, each delivering 1.5 volts, inside the metal case. These are either six flat cells or six cylindrical cells, connected in series (the positive terminal from one connects to the negative terminal of the next cell). You can see this by getting an adult to help you carefully open a 9-volt battery case and extract the six cells.

Motorboat

The Swamp Boat (page 61) and the Motor Duck DUKW (page 68) are driven by propellers spinning in the air. Their propellers spin too fast to be positioned under the water (up to 17,000 revolutions per minute, or rpm, when powered by a 9-volt battery); if you tried, water would fly everywhere. But using a lower-voltage power supply reduces the speed. One or at most two 1.5-volt batteries provide plenty of power for this boat, which has its propeller below the waterline.

Toy motors will work when they are wet. However, dunking them in water too much or storing them without drying them first will ruin them. It is best to mount the motor inside the boat where it is usually dry and extend the motor shaft through the hull to a propeller.

Adult supervision required

Materials

Milk carton hull (page 10) plus
    additional pieces of milk carton
Toy motor
Cocktail straw
Masking tape
Hot glue gun
1 or 2 AA batteries in battery pack
Knife blade switch (optional)
2 or 3 alligator clip leads

Propeller (or make your own)
Diagonal cutters (optional)
D battery (optional)
Rubber band (optional)
Aluminum foil (optional)
Pocketknife with awl (optional)

Build It

1. Use a milk carton hull and fold a rectangle of the milk carton material to prop up the motor.

2. Get an idea where the motor will be located. It will have to be angled down toward the back of the boat to get the propeller in the water. To hold the motor in position you will need to support it with some material (the folded milk carton material from step 1) and to extend the motor shaft to reach the propeller, which will be outside the boat in the water.

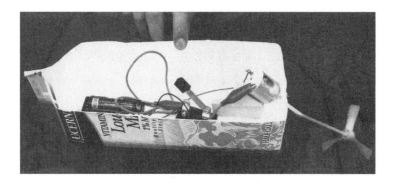

3. A cocktail straw is just slightly larger in diameter than the motor shaft and makes a good shaft extension. You can buy a box of hundreds of these at a restaurant supply store—or you can grab a handful at a cafe or restaurant with a bar. To make the straw fit snugly on the motor shaft, put one wrap of masking tape around the motor shaft and then force the straw onto the taped shaft.

4. Make a motor mount. In this model, scraps of plastic are used to hold the motor up. Note how high the angle is. This makes the propeller push water downward as well as to the rear, which wastes much of its energy. Pushing water down does not propel the boat forward. A shallower angle would deliver more forward power. Instead of plastic scraps, folded pieces of milk carton material can be hot glued to the hull for a motor mount.

5. Add power. This model uses a battery pack that holds two AA batteries; try using one battery and try using two. A knife blade switch makes it easier to operate the motor. Alligator clip leads connect the battery, switch, and motor in a series. Three clip leads are required: one lead connects one side of the battery to the switch, the next connects the other side of the battery to one terminal on the motor, and the third connects the second motor terminal to the second connection on the switch.

6. Add a propeller. The propeller in this model is the same one used for the Swamp Boat. The opening in the center of the propeller had to be reamed out with an awl so the cocktail straw could fit and be glued in. A propeller with shorter blades would work better. Later we snipped off the ends of this propeller using diagonal cutters.

7. A variation on this design uses a single D cell battery without a battery pack. The ends of the alligator clip leads are held to the battery with a thick rubber band. This is a bit awkward, but it works. The motor shaft makes a low angle into the water so the propeller can deliver most of its push to moving the boat forward. A piece of folded aluminum foil holds the motor up above the deck.

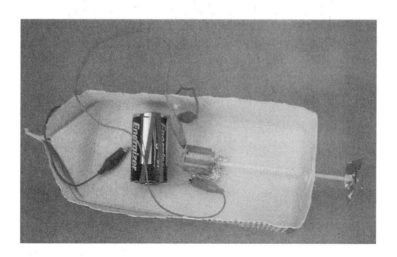

8. The propeller in this model is a piece of aluminum foil. Starting with a piece about 3 inches long by 1 inch wide, fold it twice in each direction. With an awl, poke a small hole in the center of the rectangular piece of foil and push it onto the shaft, which is a cocktail straw. Dab some hot glue to hold it in place. To get the proper *pitch* on the propeller blades (the required twist that will push water backward), hold the propeller in both hands between your thumbs and forefingers and twist your hands in opposite directions. A great feature of this homemade propeller is that you can try different pitches to see which works best.

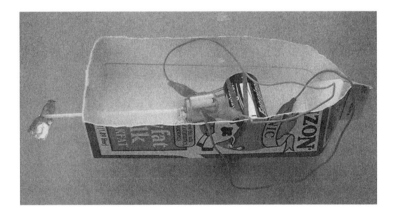

Sailing Further

If the propeller shaft is aligned along the centerline of the boat, the boat will turn to one side as it moves forward. This is the common problem with a one-motor boat. Reposition the motor to counteract this. If the boat steers to the *starboard* (that's "to the right" for you landlubbers), shift the motor to the *port* (left). With the motor pushing slightly to the port, the stern of the boat will move to the right and push the bow to the left. A keel, or skegs, made of pieces of milk carton can help too.

Ship's Log

John Ericsson is credited with inventing the ship's propeller and is recognized for this by the National Inventors Hall of Fame. Other inventors had created and patented designs before Ericsson, but success in a race pitting his propeller ship against a paddle wheel–driven ship convinced many people that propellers were superior to paddles. He later designed the Civil War–era ironclad warship the USS *Monitor*.

Ole Evinrude invented the gasoline outboard motor in 1907. The need for a boat motor became evident to him when fetching an ice cream cone for his girlfriend on a hot day. Ole had rowed across a lake to buy his girlfriend some ice cream, but by the time he returned it had melted. With that inspiration, he launched the Evinrude Motor Company. He also helped to launch a major motorcycle business by giving two young engine tinkerers, William Harley and Arthur Davidson, the opportunity to mess around in his shop.

*   *   *

Keel was possibly the first word in the English language to appear in a written document. It refers to the central structure along the length of a ship or boat, which helps it move in a straight line. In a sailboat, the keel is weighted to give the boat more stability from side to side and is usually augmented by a moveable *centerboard*, an extension that can be raised up out of the way when the boat goes into shallow water. A *skeg* is a fin mounted on the bottom of a surfboard, kayak, or other small boat to give some directional stability.

Belt Drive Boat

Belt and chain drives were prominent in the age of steam to drive vehicles and machinery in factories. They were used in gasoline-powered trucks in the early 20th century but then lost popularity. Today belt drives have made a big comeback. Jet skis and snowmobiles use them, and people are trying them in larger vehicles.

Here is a model that will inspire you to improvise your own designs once you understand the concept. Rubber bands serve as belts to carry the motor's motion to an axle that drives paddles, either on each side of the boat or at the back of the boat. The cheap, high-speed motors used in previous projects can power these boats, as shown in the first example below, but a motor with a lower rpm works better.

Adult supervision required

Materials

Dowel, ¼-inch or ⅛-inch diameter
Larger pulley to fit dowel (or 2 wooden
    wheels to serve as pulley)
Drill and bits (optional)
Smaller gear/pulley to fit motor shaft
Milk carton hull (page 10) plus
    additional pieces of milk carton
Single hole punch
Scrap paper
Pencil
Rubber bands

Toy motor
2 AA batteries
Battery case for AA batteries
2 alligator clip leads
Hot glue gun
4 craft sticks
Scissors (optional)
Solar motor (optional)
Pocketknife (optional)
2 large paper clips (optional)

Build It

1. Push the larger pulley onto the dowel, which will serve as the axle. You may have to drill the center hole in the pulley so it fits snugly onto the dowel. A rubber band looped between this pulley and one on the motor shaft will carry the motion from the motor to the paddles, which will be mounted on either side of the dowel. If you don't have a pulley, you can make one; in the model pictured here, two wooden wheels were glued together with a space between them to hold the rubber band. (In fact, you could run a rubber band directly from the motor shaft to the dowel without any pulleys, but the pulleys will help keep the rubber band from slipping.)

2. Put the smaller pulley on the motor shaft. The size difference between the pulleys helps give your motor a mechanical advantage: using a smaller pulley on the motor shaft and a larger one on the axle/dowel will lower the speed at which the axle

rotates. Going slower is an advantage, as even the slow motors spin too fast for effective paddles.

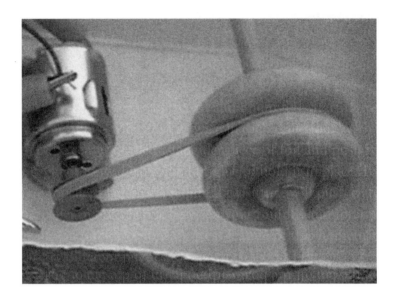

3. Next, you'll mount the axle, by sliding it between two holes on opposite sides of your milk carton hull, as shown in the completed model on page 84. Decide where you want to place the holes: If you place them too high, the paddles may not reach the water. If you place them too low, the pulley may rub on the deck. Too far to the stern and the pulley may rub against the transom.

4. Once you've found the best location, punch one hole with a hole punch. The hole punch will make holes with smooth edges that will give less friction to the spinning axle. Take some care to make the second hole at the same distance above the water and at the same distance in front of the transom as the first. One way to do this is to make a jig: Punch the first hole on one side of the boat and lay a

rectangular piece of scrap paper against that side, aligned with both the bottom of the boat and the transom. Push a pencil through the paper where the punched hole is. Now lay it against the opposite side of the boat, so the same edges are aligned with the transom and the bottom of the boat. Make a mark on the boat where it lines up with the hole in the paper; that's where you should punch the second hole.

5. Slide the axle with the pulley through one hole and loop a rubber band around the pulley. Then slide the other end of the axle through the second hole.
6. Insert two AA batteries into the battery case and connect it to the motor terminals with two alligator clip leads.
7. With the motor spinning, loop the rubber band onto the pulley on the motor shaft. Hold the motor while it spins and see how far from the axle it should be

placed to give the rubber band the correct tension. The tension has to be strong enough that the rubber band doesn't slip on either pulley but not so tight that it stops the motor from turning.

8. Mark the position of the motor on the deck where the tension seems best. With the motor disconnected from the battery, hot glue the motor on your marks.

9. Add paddles to each end of the axle. In the model shown, two craft sticks are glued to make each paddle. With the high-speed motor used in this boat, and the low drag afforded by the skinny paddle blades, these paddles spin fast.

Test It

Reconnect the battery pack to the motor with clip leads and see where the paddleboat goes.

Sailing Further

The following model is a nice upgrade. It has several advantages over the basic model just presented. First, it uses a motor that spins at one-eighth of the speed of the less expensive motor. The paddleboat works best when the paddles spin more slowly. Second, the motor is mounted so it can be moved to adjust the tension in the rubber band. Gluing the motor to the deck and having it work well while you hold it in midair but stop working when you lower it into the water can be a frustrating experience. This motor mount system lets you reposition the motor simply by sliding the motor mount forward or backward.

1. This model uses ⅛-inch dowels rather than the ¼-inch dowels used in the model on the previous pages. The smaller dowels are easier to work with, are less expensive, and fit the pulleys we had on hand. The disadvantage is that they do break, while ¼-inch dowels are much sturdier.

2. The paddles are constructed from two interlocking pieces of coated paper from a milk carton. They are as long as a half-gallon milk carton is wide: 3.5 inches. Each paddle is about 1.5 inches wide. Cut narrow slots in the middle of each blade on its long side so they can slide together to form a paddle. A bead of hot glue along the seams between the two blades of each paddle holds them in place. When the glue has cooled and hardened, place a second bead along one of the seams to attach the paddle to the axle protruding from the side of the boat.

3. Before attaching the second paddle to the axle, slide the axle through one of the holes you punched in the side of the boat. Force the pulley onto the axle and loop a rubber band around the pulley. Then slide the axle through the second hole and add the second paddle.
4. Make sure the pulley and motor are aligned. If they are not aligned, the belt may jump off.

5. Now add the motor. The model uses a low-current (0.02 amp), low-voltage (2-volt) motor, known as a solar motor. It costs four times as much as the higher-speed motors, but it is still available for under three dollars. This type of motor also works great for other projects you will read about later. The voltage required to drive a solar motor is about 2 volts. We tried using one AA battery (1.5 volts) but that was not enough, so as with the previous version, we used two AA batteries in a battery case. Rather than gluing the motor to the deck of the boat, mount it on a different piece of a milk carton.

6. To make the motor mount, use a pocketknife to cut across the side panel of another half-gallon milk carton. Extend the cut ¼ inch into each adjacent side. Repeat this cut along a parallel line about 1 inch away. You end up with a U-shaped piece of coated paper that is 1 inch wide. It sits perfectly on top of the hull. Glue the motor to this mount with the motor shaft in the middle as shown.

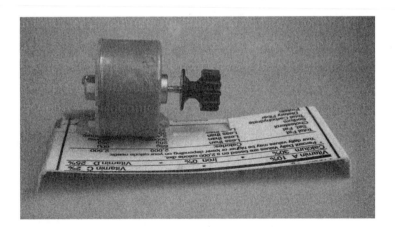

7. Loop the rubber band either around the motor shaft or, if you are using a pulley on the shaft, around the pulley. Then power up the motor.

8. Slide the motor mount back and forth toward the bow and toward the stern to find the best location where the tension in the rubber band doesn't slip on the axle pulley and where it isn't so tight that it prevents the axle from spinning. Use paper clips to hold the motor mount in this position on the hull. After testing the boat in water, you can glue the motor mount in position or continue to use clips to hold it in place. Does it work better with the pointy end forward or the flat end (transom) of the boat going forward? Reverse the connections to the battery to get the motor spinning in the opposite direction to find out.

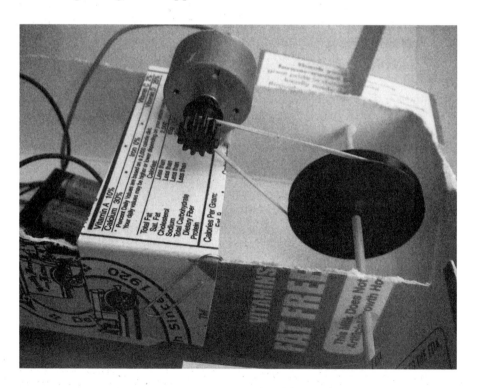

Science

Hot glue, dismissed by many people as a craft or toy tool, will help you develop new boat prototypes at the speed of ideas. Because hot glue sets so quickly, your thinking isn't delayed by waiting for it to harden. Changes, in most cases, are a wrist twist away as you rip apart a mistake and create a new design.

How does this sticky magic happen? The glue is a thermoplastic, which is a long-chain polymer that melts at relatively low temperatures (250°F for low-temperature guns and 380°F for high-temperature guns) but freezes when removed from the heat. When it freezes, it sticks. The gun is a heater that melts the glue stick and pushes out the liquid glue—hopefully not onto your fingers.

Inside the glue gun, a trigger mechanism pushes the glue stick into the heating element near the tip of the gun. Inside the heating element are two electrodes and a block of high-resistance material (6,500 ohms—I measured) that heats up when electrical current runs through it.

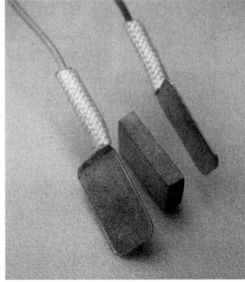

Gear Drive Boat

To make a Gear Drive Boat, replace the belt from the previous model with gears. It's not quite that simple, but almost. The belt tends to stay on the pulleys provided that they are aligned with each other and the tension is correct. The gears, however, seem to be quite happy jumping out of alignment if you allow them. You may need to add some washers or bearings to the axle to keep it from sliding from side to side, which allows the gears to release.

Adult supervision required

Materials

Dowels, ⅛-inch diameter
Larger gear to fit dowel
Smaller gear/pulley to fit motor shaft
Milk carton hull (page 10) plus additional pieces of milk carton
Single hole punch
Scrap paper
Pencil
Rubber bands
Scissors
Solar motor
2 AA batteries in battery pack
2 alligator clip leads
Pocketknife
2 large paper clips

Build It

1. This model is nearly identical to the alternate version of the Belt Drive Boat (page 85). You'll use a milk carton hull. Power comes from a pair of AA batteries held in a battery case. Connections are provided by two alligator clip leads. The motor is still glued to a motor mount that is moveable. The mount is cut from a milk carton (but could also be cut from a craft stick). Paddles are the same but have been mounted onto a new axle that has a large gear in the center instead of a pulley.

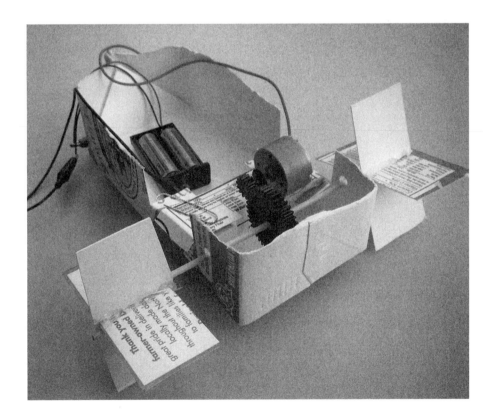

2. To get the gear on the motor shaft to fit into the gear on the drive axle, the motor has to be located lower and closer to the axle. Using the pocketknife, make two vertical cuts in both sides of the boat and bend the rectangular section of the milk carton inward. These tabs of coated paper support the motor mount and give a place to clip or clamp the mount to the boat.

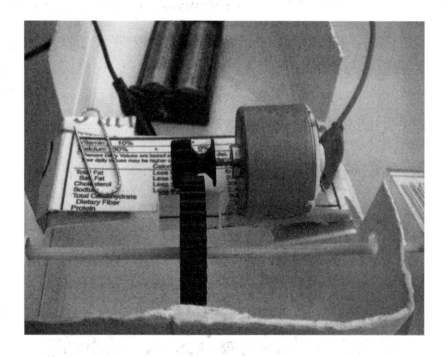

3. Place the motor mount into the slots you just cut and see if the motor gear will reach the gear on the axle. If it does, paper clip the mount to the tabs you just cut. If it doesn't, make additional cuts so it will.

Test It

With the boat elevated above a table so that the paddles can turn, connect the motor to the battery. Do the gears stay engaged? If so, put the model in your ocean for the ultimate test.

If the gears do not stay engaged, slide small paper clips onto the axle next to the holes in the side of the boat. This should allow the axle to spin freely but stop it from moving side to side.

Science

Using a small gear on the motor shaft, called a pinion or driving gear, and a larger gear on the axle, called the driven gear, slows the speed of axle rotation. If the smaller gear has 10 teeth and the larger one has 20, the gear ratio is two to one. The larger gear turns one revolution when the smaller gear makes two revolutions. Also, notice that the two gears spin in opposite directions. If the pinion gear spins clockwise, the driven gear spins counterclockwise. If for some reason both have to turn in the same direction, a third gear, called an idler gear, is inserted between them.

Find the gear ratio of your boat by counting the number of teeth on each gear. Or make a mark on each gear where the gears are touching and slowly turn the pinion gear while counting the number of partial or full revolutions it makes before the mark on the larger gear comes back to the starting position.

Water Jet Boat

Personal watercraft and some larger boats are propelled by water jets. An advantage of using jet drive is that there is no propeller to hit rocks in shallow water or people who have fallen overboard.

Water jet boats use submersible, battery-powered pumps to drive them. Pumps are not as easy to find as electric motors are, so you will learn how to make them in chapter 4 (page 134). Battery-operated pumps are available either from science supply companies or from garden and hardware stores that sell small, inexpensive fountains.

Adult supervision required

Materials

Styrene plate or milk carton hull (page 10)
Submersible pump
9-volt battery
Drinking straws, milkshake/fat size, or
    similarly sized vinyl tubing
Hot glue gun
2 alligator clip leads
Scissors
Pocketknife
Rubber band

Build It

1. Model 1. The first model shown here has an inexpensive pump mounted in the center of a styrene plate. The water discharged by the pump goes overboard through the vinyl tubing. A 9-volt battery powers the pump, connected via two alligator clip leads. There are two holes cut into the hull with scissors, one on the underside so the pump can suck water and the other on the side for the tube to release the water overboard. Both leak. The deck is flooded. It is hard to solve this problem by using a hot glue gun to fill the holes because the styrene melts at about 40°F, below the temperature at which the hot glue does. Holding a hot glue gun, even a low-temperature gun, against styrene melts it and makes a bigger hole. Keeping the gun away from the styrene, you can carefully dribble hot glue to fill in the openings.

2. Model 2. A better approach is to use a milk carton hull. This first milk carton model has the pump mounted in the bow with a milkshake straw to guide the discharge out the back, through a hole cut in the transom with a pocketknife. (This model has a backup propeller motor mounted on the transom, above the tube.)

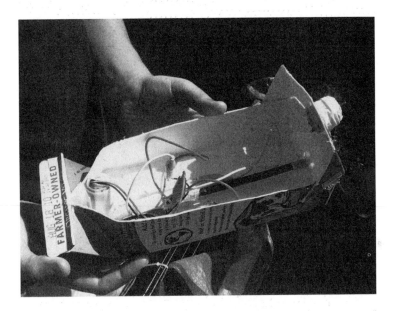

3. Model 3. Another milk carton design uses a large pump from a garden fountain. Because this pump draws water from below, it had to be set into the deck of the boat. To cut the hole in the hull, place the pump on the underside of the boat and trace it. Cut out this rectangle with a pocketknife so the pump can be squeezed in. Use a bead of hot glue to form a seal between the pump and the hull. Powered by a 9-volt battery, the pump draws water up through vents in its base, which is now underwater. It pushes the water out the top and into the vinyl tube, which carries

it overboard. The direction can be changed by moving the tube, which is held in place under a rubber band, to either side.

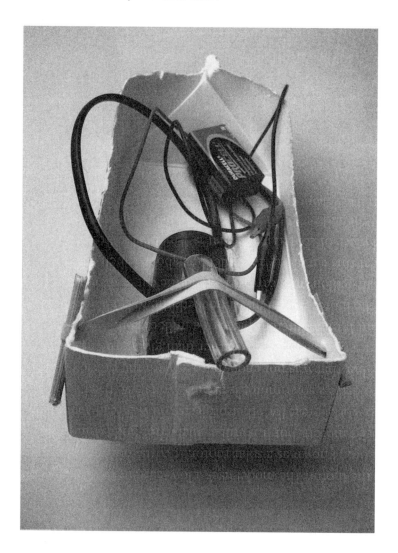

4. Model 4. One more milk carton design uses an outboard pump motor hung onto the transom. It is glued to the transom low enough so it can suck up water from below and pump it out the back. This model is easy to make and works very well.

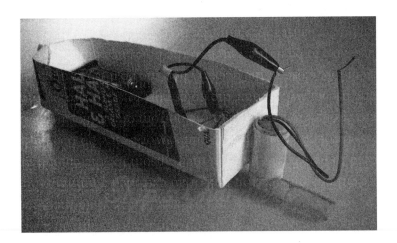

5. Model 5. A different approach is to use the pump to feed water into a Gravity-Powered Boat (page 33). As long as the pump moves water at about the same rate as water empties from the cup, this approach works well. You can adjust the flow by using a narrower or larger discharge tube or straw.

Ship's Log

In the late 19th century and the first decade of the 20th century, electric boats were popular. They lost their popularity when internal combustion engines became available. Today electric motors are used by fishermen for slow, quiet trolling and are used in environmentally sensitive areas to prevent oil or gasoline from leaking into the water. Tugboats and ships are increasingly using electric drive motors, supplied by diesel generators.

Solar-Powered Boat

Having an electric boat operate without a battery is pretty cool. It can splash around a sunny pool or ocean all day long at no expense.

Adult supervision required

Materials

Milk carton hull (page 10) plus
    additional pieces of milk carton for paddles
Scissors
Hot glue gun
2 gear wheels
Drinking straw
Dowel, ⅛-inch diameter
Solar motor
1 or more solar cells
3 alligator clip leads
Sunlight

Build It

1. One approach to making a solar-powered boat is to start with either the Belt Drive Boat (page 80) or the Gear Drive Boat (page 90) and replace the battery with solar cells. Depending on the output of the solar cells you use, you might

need to reduce the size of the paddles or use multiple solar cells connected in series to generate higher voltages.

2. Here is a different design to build. Rather than make paddles from intersecting pieces of milk carton, use scissors to cut out four rectangular milk carton pieces, notch and fold them as shown, and hot glue them to two gear wheels. The wheels actually serve two purposes: not only do they hold the paddle blades, but one of them meshes with the pinion gear on the motor shaft.

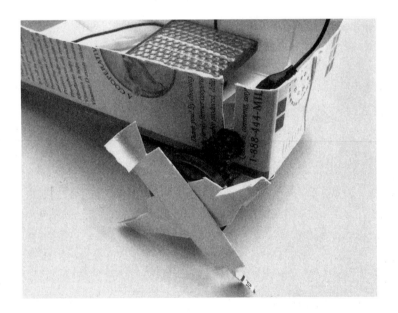

3. To build the rest of the boat above, start by hot gluing a drinking straw to the bottom of the hull, with the openings on the sides where you want the paddles to be. Insert an ⅛-inch-diameter dowel into the straw to serve as the axle, and mount the gear wheels with the paddle blades on either end.

4. Mount a solar motor inside the boat, directly above one of the gear wheels. Cut a slot in the side of the boat to allow the motor shaft to stick through the hull and reach one of the gear wheels. To hold the motor in position, glue it either to the hull or to a folded piece of milk carton that is glued to the hull.

5. Lay a solar cell in the boat where it can catch the sun's rays. If the sun is at a low angle, prop up the solar cell on a piece of folded milk carton so it can better capture the rays. Make sure that nothing gets in front of the cell that could block the rays.

Test It

On a sunny day, a single solar panel can power the motor. Use alligator clip leads to connect the motor's terminals to the terminals on the solar panel. Reverse the leads to get the motor to spin in the opposite direction.

Sailing Further

For better performance, two solar cells can be connected in series. That is, one alligator clip lead connects the positive terminal of one solar cell to the negative terminal on the second cell. Two more clip leads connect the remaining two solar cell terminals to the two terminals on the motor. See the recommendations for purchasing solar cells in appendix A (page 217).

Ship's Log

Solar-powered boats aren't just models. Some modern solar boats stretch over 100 feet in length and are ocean-going craft.

Ship's Chandlery

When purchasing solar cells, check the specifications for output voltage and current. Compare the solar cell specifications to those for the motors you will use. If the motor requires 2 volts or more, you will have to connect two or more solar cells in series. See appendix A (page 217) for more suggestions.

Rainy Day Solar-Powered Boat

An interesting addition to your solar model makes it work on rainy days and highlights the central issue for relying on solar and wind energy: how do you store the energy? Green energy is great, but what do you do with the excess energy you collect when you don't need it? And where do you get energy when the sun isn't shining and the wind isn't blowing?

On the size scale of models, the answer is a supercapacitor (more correctly called an electric double-layer capacitor). This is a new technology that allows electric charges to be stored physically—no chemical reaction as in batteries—at energy densities hundreds of times higher than traditional capacitors. Supercapacitors are available only at science supply stores and in catalogs.

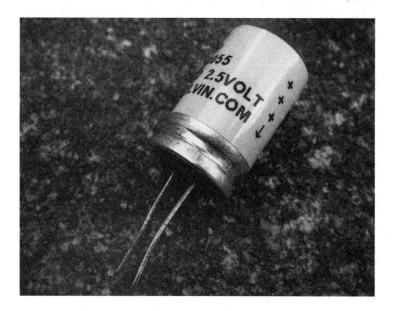

Materials

Solar-Powered Boat (page 100)
2.5-volt supercapacitor (10 or 20 farads)
Sunlight
Voltmeter or solar motor (optional)
2 alligator clip leads (optional)

Build It

1. Start with the solar-powered boat from the preceding project and remove the solar cells.
2. Use the solar cells to charge up a supercapacitor. Connect the positive terminal of the capacitor to the positive terminal of a solar cell or the positive terminal of an array of solar cells. Connect the negative terminal of the capacitor to the negative side of the solar cell or array.
3. Expose the solar cells to sunlight. In direct sunlight the capacitor will charge in a few minutes. If it is raining outside, charge the capacitor indoors with the solar cells under a high-wattage light, making sure you don't melt the plastic in the solar cells. This will take longer than charging the capacitor with sunlight.
4. Monitor the charging progress with a voltmeter or with a solar motor. Measure the DC voltage in the capacitor after a few minutes of charging and compare that to the specified voltage on the side of the capacitor. Or, use alligator clip leads to connect the capacitor terminals to a solar motor and see when it has charged enough to spin the motor. (Unlike NiCad rechargeable batteries, super-capacitors do not lose potential charging capacity if you recharge them before they are fully drained.)

Test It

Insert the charged supercapacitor into the boat's circuit where the solar panels were in the previous project. To do this, use alligator clip leads to connect one leg of the capacitor to one of the terminals on the motor. Then connect the other leg to the other terminal. Place the boat in the water and watch it go. With a full charge, a supercapacitor will drive the boat for several minutes.

Steamboat

Until the 1970s, most large ships were powered by steam. Giant boilers burned "bunker" fuel to heat water in pipes. The resulting steam could drive either reciprocating engines, which used pistons moving up and down, or steam turbines. Today most ships use diesel engines, and some naval ships burn gas to spin turbines. A few ships use steam where nuclear reactions, rather than burning bunker oil, provide the source of heat.

Another type of steamboat uses a unique drive system: putt-putt boats. These are too inefficient to use in commerce, but in your backyard pool they are wonderful.

Putt-putt boats use a steam engine with no moving parts. You fill a boiler with water and heat the boiler with a small candle.

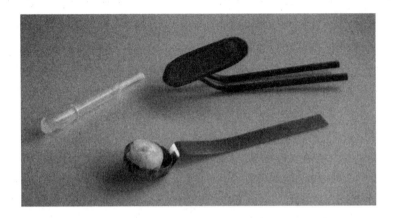

The temperature of the water rises and, after a minute or so, exceeds the boiling point. Some of the water vaporizes instantly into steam, which dramatically increases the pressure inside the boiler. Since steam, the vapor or gas form of water, takes up much more volume than water does, the pressure inside the boiler increases as water changes to steam. An explosive pulse of steam pushes the remaining water out two exhaust tubes. The boat moves forward. Steam remaining in the boiler quickly condenses, drawing water back into the tubes and refilling the boiler, which is still being heated by the candle, so the cycle repeats as long as the candle is burning.

On every cycle the engine emits a "putt-putt" sound as steam forces water out and then draws water back into the tubes. You can also hear a clicking sound on each cycle as the flexible diaphragm in the motor moves up as water flashes into steam and then down as the steam and water rush out the exhaust. After a few minutes the candle burns down and goes out, and with no source of heat, the boat stops.

There has been some debate on how these boats operate. We know they move, but few people agree on why. Dr. Alejandro Jenkins at Florida State University sent me several papers he has published on the physics of putt-putt boats. I rely on his analysis to describe the process.

Most physicists agree with the description of how the motors push water out the exhaust. It's what happens next that causes disagreement. I will stick with Dr. Jenkins. As the steam leaves the boiler, the now low pressure in the boiler draws water back into the tube. Shouldn't this returning water cancel out the forward thrust of the discharging water? Obviously it doesn't, because the boat moves forward. Some of the boat's forward momentum is lost when it draws water into the tubes, but that momentum is regained as the incoming water's momentum is transferred to the tubes, pushing the boat forward. The net effect of drawing water into the engine is that you barely notice a loss of forward momentum and motion. It seems weird that you blow water out to move forward, but drawing water back in doesn't pull the boat back.

Jearl Walker's classic book *The Flying Circus of Physics* provides a different explanation. According to him, when the water is blasted out, it is pushed directly behind the boat. But when it is drawn into the tubes, it comes from all sides surrounding the tubes. Thus the push is focused in one direction while the pull is spread out in many different directions, so the push is stronger. You can choose which one you want to believe or come up with your own hypothesis. The world of science awaits your analysis.

You can buy putt-putt boats made of tin at maritime museums, festivals, and toy stores, or from science catalogs. Or, you can buy just the engines (from science catalogs) and create your own. A third option is to coil copper tubing around a form to make a boiler. This option is more difficult and the resulting engine doesn't work as well, so it's probably best to just purchase a steam engine.

Materials

Milk carton hull (page 10) or extruded aluminum hull (page 17)
Single hole punch or awl
Miniature steam engine, with candle and
  eyedropper to fill the exhaust tubes
Hot glue gun
Matches

Build It

1. You can use either a milk carton hull or an extruded aluminum hull. For either one, you need to punch two holes in the transom for the engine suction/discharge tubes to pass through. A single hole punch works fine on the aluminum but may not be sharp enough to get through the bottom of a milk carton. If a hole punch doesn't work, use an awl. Center the holes port to starboard on the transom and position them low, close to the deck. When the boat is running, the ends of the engine tubes have to be in the water, so the holes need to be close to the water.

2. Slide the engine exhaust tubes into the holes and use hot glue to make seals around the tubes. This will prevent water from coming into the boat and sinking it. Hot glue may not seem like a good choice for a steam engine since it is thermoplastic and could melt if the tubes get hot enough. But hot glue melts at a much higher temperature than the boiling point of water. Also, the tubes are transporting cool water on every pulse of the engine cycle, so the glue won't melt from the engine's heat. The glue that seals the holes in the transom should hold up the engine high enough so the tiny candle that comes with the engine can fit under it.

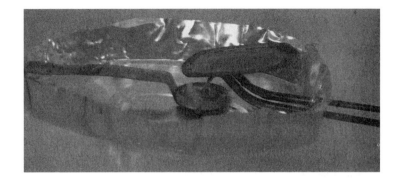

Test It

Also included when you buy the engine is a small squeeze dropper. Use this to pump water into one of the tubes. Hold the tubes vertically with the openings up, and squeeze enough water into one tube that it comes out the other tube. Put the boat in the water and add fuel.

Place a candle in the holder and light it with a match. Use the holder to slide the burning candle under the engine. In seconds you will hear the putt-putt sounds and see the boat motor around your ocean.

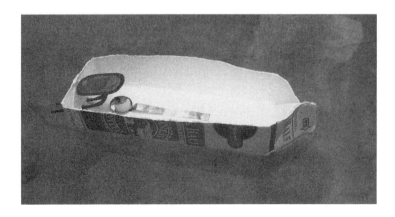

Ship's Log

Facing the bow on a ship or boat, the left side is called *port* and the right *starboard*. Using words other than *left* and *right* makes sense, since what was the left side becomes the right side when you face aft. But why call the left *port* and right *starboard*?

Before midship rudders were invented in the 12th century, sailors steered boats with steering oars mounted on one side of the hull, near the stern. Since most people are right-handed, the steering oars were located on the right side of the ship. This steering side was called starboard. The opposite side was the *larboard*.

But the similar sounding names were confusing, so sailors started calling the left side of the ship *port*. Port was an obvious choice since the left side of the ship was tied up to the dock to keep the steering oar on the starboard side from being damaged by bumping the dock and ship.

Pneumatic Jet Boat

In balloon-powered boats, propulsion energy is stored in an inflated balloon. Another way to store energy is to increase the pressure in a nonflexible container. A scuba tank, for instance, holds over 2,000 pounds per square inch of compressed air. That pressure forces air out when the valve is opened.

Here is an air pressure boat that stores energy at much lower air pressure. The storage container is a one-liter water bottle. Even at low pressure it will hold an impressive amount of energy.

Adult supervision required

Materials

Milk carton hull (page 10) plus
   additional pieces of milk carton for fins
1-liter plastic water bottle with cap
Scissors
Duct tape
Hot glue gun
Drill and $\frac{5}{64}$-inch bit
Floor-stand bicycle pump with pressure gauge
Basketball inflating needle
Silly Putty or chewing gum
A helper
Drinking straw (optional)
String (optional)

Build It

1. Construction is simple. Mount the empty one-liter plastic bottle in the milk carton hull with the cap of the bottle facing aft. Duct tape will keep it in place.
2. Add some skegs, fins, or a keel to the boat to keep it going in a straight line. Cut these out of another milk carton and use hot glue to hold them in place.

3. Remove the cap from the bottle and drill a tiny hole in the center of the cap. Screw the cap back on the bottle, and you are ready to launch.

Test It

To pressurize the bottle, use a bicycle pump with a basketball inflating needle. The pump should be a floor-stand model that will allow you to add lots of air quickly, and it should have a pressure gauge so you can see how much pressure you're pumping in.

The needle will fit the hole in the bottle cap snugly. To provide a seal, wrap a piece of Silly Putty (or chewing gum) around the base of the basketball needle. Insert the needle into the pump valve and hold the valve firmly in one hand. Hold the bottle and boat in the other hand while your helper operates the pump.

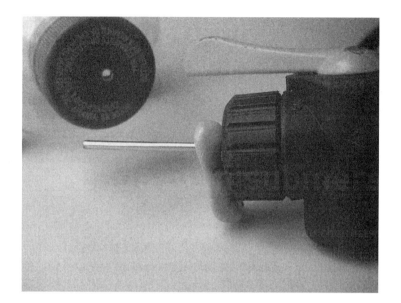

As the air pressure rises it will eventually blow holes in the Silly Putty. This pressure safety valve won't let you pump up the pressure any higher, so put the boat in the water. Remove the needle from the cap and release the boat.

Air will jet out for several seconds, plenty of time for the boat to move across a small ocean or, more likely, to make several circles. The challenge with this model is getting it to go in a straight line. If your model did not, try adding more fins.

Sailing Further

This design also makes a great rocket on a string—above your ocean or alongside of it. Tape a straw to the bottle so the straw is aligned with the length of the bottle. Pass a string through the straw and secure the string at each end, adding as much tension to the string as possible. Pump up the bottle as described above and let it zip across the string.

Chemically Powered Boats

Two household chemicals are safe propellants for boats. The first model uses Alka-Seltzer or similar products to create carbon dioxide gas when the solid tablet is dissolved in liquid water. The second model uses that common kitchen chemistry reaction of baking soda and vinegar.

Plop Plop, Fizz Fizz Skiff

This model scoots across the water surface but soon runs out of fizz. You can test the optimal quantity of fuel to use in the container.

Adult supervision required

Materials

Scissors
Styrene meat tray
Film canister (35 mm) with lid
Drill and bits or thumbtack
Hot glue gun
Water
Alka-Seltzer tablet, broken into
    halves or thirds

Build It

1. Cut a small notch in the middle of one of the short sides of a styrene meat tray. This will let the exhaust from the engine empty into the water and not onto the deck of the skiff.

2. In the side near the bottom of a 35 mm film canister, poke a hole with a thumbtack or drill the smallest hole you can—about $\frac{1}{16}$ inch.
3. Hot glue the canister to the styrene tray, cap up, with the hole pointing aft.

Test It

To test your skiff, fill the canister with water while covering the hole with your finger. Drop in a third or half a tablet of Alka-Seltzer and quickly put the lid on the canister. Release the skiff in your ocean.

The water allows the chemicals in the tablet to react with each other, producing carbon dioxide gas. Since gas takes up much more space than do liquids or solids, the pressure in the closed canister rises and pushes water out the hole. The water jet coming out of the canister pushes the boat forward.

Science

Do not launch these chemically powered models in a natural pond. You don't want to introduce foreign pollutants into the water.

Baking Soda Semisubmersible

The baking soda and vinegar reaction is legendary among home chemists for making both rockets and erupting volcanoes. In the 1940s, toy boats were propelled using this reaction. Here that design is reintroduced, but you make it at home. This model doesn't ride on the surface and doesn't go completely beneath the surface, so it is a semisubmersible.

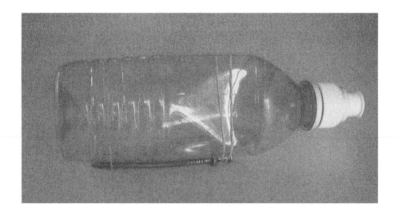

Materials

Thumbtack or drill bit
Disposable plastic water bottle with cap
Nail
Rubber bands
Water
A helper
Vinegar
Baking soda

Build It

1. Use either a thumbtack or a very small drill bit (1/16 inch) to poke a tiny hole in the bottom of a disposable water bottle. A larger hole will release the exhaust without driving the boat forward.
2. Add some weight to the boat to keep it upright. In the model shown on the previous page we used one large nail and held it in place with two rubber bands.
3. Fill the bottle halfway with water. Add about one-quarter bottle's worth of vinegar to the bottle. A helper can hold the bottle with his or her finger covering the hole so the liquid doesn't drain.
4. Now the tricky part. Put some baking soda in the cap of the bottle, filling it about halfway. Tilt the bottle so it is as close to being horizontal without spilling the liquid. Screw on the cap tightly and quickly put the semisubmersible in the water.

Test It

In seconds, carbon dioxide bubbles and water will come squirting out the back, propelling the semisubmersible forward. The vinegar and baking soda mix to produce carbon dioxide gas, which takes up much more space than did either of those two nongaseous ingredients. As the gas forms, it increases the pressure inside the sealed bottle and pushes water (and vinegar) out the hole.

Ship's Log

In marine industries, a *semisubmersible* is a vessel used for drilling in the ocean floor, most often searching for oil and gas. The semisubmersible can be raised or lowered in the water by removing or adding water to its ballast tanks. When it is low in the water it is a stable platform for working at sea.

Adjustable Rudder

An adjustable rudder would be a great addition to the Swamp Boat (page 61) or any other boat. It allows you to change the direction of the boat as you please.

Adult supervision required

Materials

> Hot glue gun
> Drinking straw, regular or milkshake
> Scissors
> Dowel, 1½ inches long, ⅛-inch or
>   ¼-inch diameter
> Smaller dowel piece to serve as the tiller
> Milk carton made of coated paper

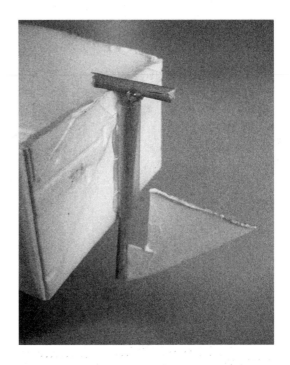

Build It

1. One way to make a rudder is to glue a short section of a straw onto the transom, the back part of the boat. The straw should be centered port to starboard and vertically. This becomes the *gudgeon* (the tube part of the rudder hinge) that holds the *pintle*, or pin, of the rudder.

2. Use the 1½-inch piece of ⅛-inch-diameter dowel for the pintle.
3. Cut the rudder out of a milk carton so it can attach to the bottom of the pintle. You can experiment with different rudder shapes, but a 1-inch-tall triangle will work nicely.
4. Hot glue the rudder to the pintle as shown. Then slide the pintle into the gudgeon from below and glue a *tiller*, or handle, to the rudder using an even smaller piece of dowel.

Sailing Further

This rudder uses a drinking straw and a ⅛-inch-diameter dowel. Use a milkshake straw and a ¼-inch dowel for a more robust version.

4

Pump It Up: Move Some Water

Moving water from one place to another is an age-old challenge for technology. Thousands of designs of pumps have been created to solve the problem. At home, in the car, and at work or school, we use dozens of pumps every day.

Take Apart a Pump

To get an idea of how pumps work, take one apart. Here are a few pumps that are easy to take apart so you can examine their inner workings.

Water Pistol

Supermarkets and toy stores sell water pistols for a couple of dollars. The easiest to disassemble are those that are held together with screws. A Phillips screwdriver is the only tool needed to get inside. Before taking the pistol apart, try it. Fill it with water and give a squirt. Can you figure out how it works?

Adult supervision required

Materials

Water pistol
Phillips screwdriver or rotary cutting tool
Adult helper
Safety glasses
Flathead screwdriver
   (to pry open the two halves)

Unbuild It

1. If the water pistol isn't held together with screws, an adult will have to help you cut it open. The best tool for this is a small, handheld rotary cutting tool. Your helper should cut along the seam that separates the left and right halves of the gun, *but should not cut through the nozzle*. Cut up to the nozzle on each side so it remains intact. Also cut the trigger guard, but don't cut through the trigger. Your helper should ***be careful cutting the plastic***, as it is easy to slip and cut a finger or hand. Also, ***do the cutting while wearing safety glasses and in a well-ventilated space*** so no one inhales the tiny bits of plastic that come flying out during the cutting.

2. Whether you separate the two halves by removing screws or cutting, lay down the gun and lift off the half that is on top. You may need to pry the two halves apart at the nozzle and anywhere else you weren't able to cut between them. Use a small flathead screwdriver.

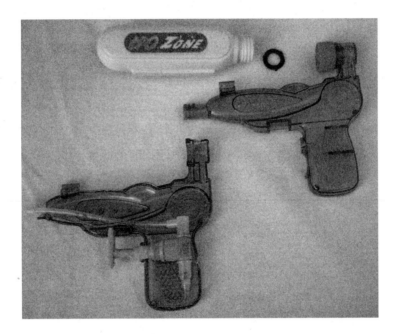

Test It

The model shown here is a common design, although most don't have the extra water reservoir on top. When you fill the gun, water occupies the entire interior of the gun.

Pulling the trigger reduces the size of the plastic chamber (to the right of the trigger), forcing water to move either upward or downward. The volume of water can't get smaller (see the "Science" section on page 127), so it has to go somewhere. Where it goes is deter-mined by the position of the two black rubber stoppers that form the two valves.

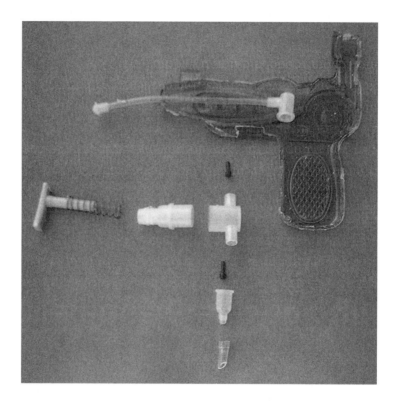

In the valve on the top, the rubber stopper lifts up, allowing water to pass as you pull the trigger. The stopper in the bottom valve is pushed into its "seat" where it blocks water flowing back into the interior of the gun. The slug of water now captured in the chamber moves up the narrow tube and out the nozzle.

Releasing the trigger allows the now compressed spring mounted on the trigger to push the trigger back out. This increases the volume of the chamber and lowers the pressure. The top stopper is sucked down into its seat and blocks any water from coming back into the chamber from the narrow tube above. The bottom stopper is lifted off its seat, allowing water to come into the chamber from the interior of the gun. This water replaces the slug of water that you just shot.

This is called a *positive displacement pump*. It holds a quantity of water and displaces it into the discharge tube. It requires a source of energy—in this case, your forefinger—and valves to control the flow. Now you give it a try.

Science

Water is nearly incompressible. No matter how much pressure you exert on it, it occupies nearly the same volume. If you took a plastic bag that was completely full of seawater at the surface and swam down 2.5 miles, you'd note that the bag was still more than 98 percent full. The water had compressed less than 2 percent, while the pressure at that depth was 400 times higher than the pressure at the surface.

Air, on the other hand, is highly compressible; you can squeeze a lot of air into a small volume under great pressure. If, after your first swim down to 2.5 miles deep, you still had some energy left, you could take down the same plastic bag completely filled with air. At the bottom the bag would appear to be empty as the air inside would have been compressed to 0.017 percent of its original volume.

Scuba divers are very aware of the difference in compressibility of air and water. Although their bodies are composed largely of water (about 70 percent), their lungs are elastic bags of compressible air. If a diver were to fill her lungs with air from a scuba tank at a 100-foot depth and swim to the surface, most of her body would be fine, but her lungs would burst long before surfacing.

Hand Pump

You probably have several of these pumps in your home. They come on bottles of hand soap, moisturizer, salad dressing, and other liquid products. Don't throw away the pump when you've used up the product—take it apart! Here is the hand pump from a liquid soap container.

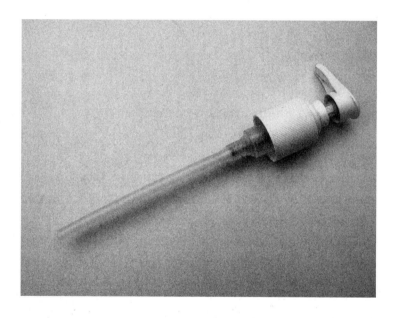

Adult supervision required

Materials

Discarded hand pump
Pliers
Cutting tools (optional)

Unbuild It

Some plastic hand pumps are difficult to pull apart. You might have to cut them apart with a knife or rotary cutting tool. This one pulled apart. Yank off the handle and pull the long fill tube off the pump. Pull the rest of the components apart.

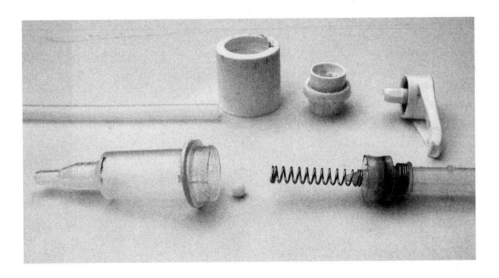

Science

Pumping down on the handle reduces the volume of room in the clear plastic chamber that holds soap. The soap, mostly water, doesn't compress so it has to go somewhere. The way down, back into the bottle, is blocked by a white ball. The only escape is up, out the tube in the handle. When you let up on the handle, the spring pushes the handle and the volume of the plastic chamber enlarges. This creates low fluid pressure in the chamber and the ball lifts off its seat, allowing more soap to enter the chamber.

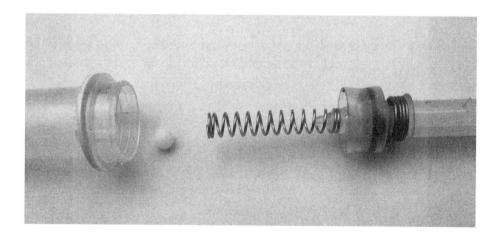

Electric Pump

Here is a small pump used to move water in a tabletop fountain. It uses a direct current motor from a power supply plugged into the wall outlet.

Adult supervision required

Materials

Diagonal cutters
Mini fountain pump from science catalog
   or home furnishings store
Phillips screwdriver

Unbuild It

1. Use diagonal cutters to remove the electrical plug and throw it away. Four screws hold the pump assembly together and attach it to the motor. Removing the screws allows the pump to come off the motor in two pieces. The bottom piece holds two gears/impellers that mesh together.

2. The motor shaft fits into one of the two and spins it. This gear spins the other gear/impeller in the opposite direction. As the gears turn, their teeth act as impeller blades, pushing water from the inlet to the discharge side. A gasket and the two impeller/gears fall out when the housing is held upside down.

3. A second plastic housing separates the motor from the lower housing holding
    the impellers. Its purpose is to make a watertight compartment for the pump to
    operate in and to keep water away from the motor.

Going Further

There are lots of other pumps that you can take apart. Keep looking for possible candi-
dates. But before you disassemble something, ***make sure that the owner has given you per-
mission and that you have removed any electrical plugs***, to prevent anyone from trying to
plug the disassembled item back in. Here are a few possibilities:

-   **Electric bubble gun:** The electric motor operates both the fan to blow bubbles
    and a *peristaltic pump* to move the bubble solution from the jar to the blower.
    (You can find more details, including photographs, in my book *Unscrewed*.)

Peristaltic pumps squeeze the flexible container holding the fluid to get it to move. Earthworms move using peristaltic contractions of muscles to lengthen and shorten their bodies.

- **Espresso machine:** The pump inside an espresso machine moves water into the reservoir. It is a *shuttle pump*. A metal shuttle inside the tube is pushed side to side by an external magnetic field. Each movement pumps up the pressure in the heating chamber. (See my book *The Way Kitchens Work* for photos and details.)
- **Bicycle pump:** In a bicycle pump, you push down on a piston that is inside a cylinder. The piston compresses air in the cylinder and forces it out, into the tire. One valve allows air to move from the upper cylinder into the compression chamber inside the cylinder, but doesn't let air escape from the compressing chamber when you are pumping downward. A second valve prevents air from coming back into the compression chamber from the tire. The tire also has its own valve that keeps air in the tube unless you manually open the valve.

Make a Pump

Pumps are more common than you might think. A car has a fuel pump, a water pump, and a windshield fluid pump, plus pumps for brakes, power steering, and maybe even a turbocharger to pump air into the engine. Your body has pumps for moving blood and fluids and for pushing foods through your digestive system.

Here is your opportunity to make a few pumps.

Baster Pump

An easy pump to make starts with a turkey baster. Ask the cook in your family if you can have it.

Adult supervision required

Materials

Plastic turkey baster
Awl
Pocketknife or ⅜-inch drill bit
Vinyl tubing, 1 foot long, ⅜-inch inside diameter
Steel ball, ½-inch diameter (from a hardware store)
Bucket of water
Scissors
Balloon, 12-inch diameter
Rubber band

Build It

1. Pop the bulb off the baster's plastic cylinder.
2. Use an awl to make a hole in the side of the bulb and then enlarge the hole with either a drill bit or a pocketknife. The hole must be large enough so you can force in a short section of vinyl tubing.

3. Insert the vinyl tubing. The fit should be quite snug.

4. Drop a steel ball into the tube. The ball needs to fit easily down the tube but stop where the tube constricts at the tip.
5. Put the bulb back on the cylinder and prepare to pump.

Test It

To operate the pump, put the tip of the plastic cylinder into a bucket of water. Squeeze the bulb but don't release it. Block any air from entering the bulb through the vinyl tube by covering the end of the tube with your finger.

Now release your grip on the bulb. As the bulb re-inflates, it will draw water up from the bucket.

Once the bulb has re-inflated, remove your finger and squeeze again. Again, cover the end of the tube and release your grip on the bulb, holding your finger in place.

It will take three or four cycles of squeezing and releasing to draw water up into the bulb before the squeezes squirt water out the tube.

Going Further

This is a two-valve pump, and so far you've made only one valve. Your finger worked as the second valve. Now you can add a second valve that will make the pumping easier. Cut the neck off of a latex balloon. Keep the round part; you will use that to make the next pump.

Pull the rolled edge of the balloon onto the vinyl tubing that is the discharge tube. Use a rubber band to hold the balloon neck in place. The end of the balloon will open to discharge water and close to prevent air from coming in during the suction cycle.

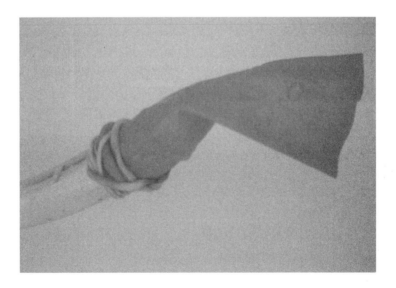

Now you have a two-valve pump. Pump on!

Diaphragm Pump

No turkey baster? No problem. Just use another kitchen tool to make a pump. This time on your way through the kitchen, grab a plastic funnel.

This pump works the same way as the Baster Pump. The difference is that with this model you have to make the bulb.

Adult supervision required

Materials

Awl
Plastic funnel
Knife
Vinyl tubing, ⅜-inch inside diameter
Hot glue gun
Steel ball, ½-inch diameter (from a hardware store)
Balloon, 12-inch diameter
Scissors
Rubber band
Bucket of water

Build It

1. Use the awl to cut a hole in the side of a funnel for the discharge tube. (The plastic used in funnels shatters easily if you try drilling through it with a twist bit instead.) Then use a sturdy knife blade to make the hole large enough so a short

piece of vinyl tube can squeeze in. Seal the joint between the tube and funnel with hot glue.

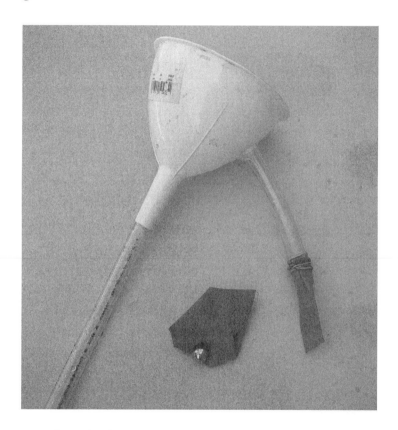

2. Fit a section of vinyl tube to the bottom of the funnel. This is the supply side of the pump.
3. Drop a steel ball into the funnel. The ball should be large enough to cover the top of the tube and not fall out the bottom. The ball makes a valve to block water from falling back into the bucket.

4. If you have the other piece of a balloon from the Baster Pump project (page 135), use that now. Otherwise, cut the neck off a balloon and stretch the other piece over the top of the funnel. This is the diaphragm.
5. Add the second valve on the discharge side as in the Baster Pump. This valve is the neck of the balloon, held in place with a rubber band.

Test It

To operate the pump, grab a bit of the balloon diaphragm and pull it up. This will draw water up the feed tube.

The upward-flowing water pushes the steel ball out of its seat. As soon as the water stops moving upward, the steel ball falls back into place, blocking any water from leaving. Meanwhile, the balloon valve on the discharge side closes, preventing air from coming in there.

Push the diaphragm down. This pushes air out the discharge side. When you let the diaphragm back up, water will well up into the funnel from the tube below. Repeat this pumping process a few more times to "prime" the pump or get enough water into the pump so it can start pumping water out. Once the water level has risen to the height of the hole for discharge, water will start coming out.

Electric Pump

Instead of relying on your muscle to operate the pump, make a pump powered by an electric battery. This pump is a *velocity pump* or *dynamic pump*. By spinning the water it increases the pressure in a container, forcing water out the discharge side.

A 35 mm film canister is the housing for this pump. The design concept is that the pump will draw in water through the hole in the bottom of the canister, spin the water, and force it out the vinyl tube near the top. Use an inexpensive toy motor to spin the water.

Adult supervision required

Materials

Drill and bits
Film canister (35 mm) or other small cylindrical container with lid
Single hole punch
Vinyl tubing, ⅛-inch inside diameter
Hot glue gun
Hacksaw or rotary cutting tool
Adult helper
Toy motor
Gear/pulley to fit motor shaft
Milk carton made of coated paper
Scissors
Dowel, ½ inch long, ¼-inch diameter (optional)
Vise (optional)
2 alligator clip leads
2 AA batteries in battery pack

Build It

1. Drill a ¼-inch hole in the bottom of a 35 mm film canister.
2. Drill or use a hole punch to cut a hole in the side of the canister, ½ inch from the top. Insert a piece of vinyl tubing into this hole and hot glue it into place. The tubing is the discharge side of the pump, so you can make this tube as long as you need to reach wherever you want the water to go. Tubing with ¼-inch outer diameter is sold as ⅛-inch (inside diameter) tubing at hardware stores.

3. Use a small drill bit to make a hole centered in the film canister lid. A common motor shaft size for inexpensive motors is 2 mm. For this size use a ⁵⁄₆₄-inch bit. Check the fit to see that the motor shaft will just barely fit through.
4. The most difficult step in building this motor is making the impeller. It needs to be exactly centered on the motor shaft. The model shown here uses a plastic

gear/pulley to hold the impeller blade. The value of using the gear/pulley is that it fits snugly and symmetrically on the shaft and, since it is made of plastic, is easy to mount an impeller blade to.

I used a hacksaw to cut a slot in the top of the gear/pulley directly across the center. I cut a piece of milk carton about 1¼ inches long and ½ inch wide. Dribbling some molten glue into the slot, I pushed the milk carton impeller blade into the slot.

5. Up to this point there is no need to ensure that the two arms of the impeller blade are the same length. By cutting the milk carton longer than it needs to be, you can now trim it to fit into the film canister. What if you don't have a gear/pulley or other component that fits snugly onto the motor shaft? Make one from a piece of wood or plastic. For instance, you can use a ½-inch-long piece of a ¼-inch-diameter dowel. Holding the dowel in a vise, carefully drill a ⁵⁄₆₄-inch-diameter hole into which the motor shaft will fit. Have an adult helper use a rotary cutting tool or hacksaw to cut a slot in the other end of the dowel to hold the impeller blade. Lather the motor shaft with hot glue and force the dowel onto the shaft. Then add the impeller blade as described above.

6. Assemble the components. Put the cap on the canister, with the motor on the outside and the impeller on the inside. Push down to make sure the cap is snugly on.

Test It

With the pump submerged in water, use the alligator clip leads to connect the motor to a battery pack with two AA batteries. In just a second, water will squirt out the vinyl tube.

Going Further

With your pump working well, revisit two earlier projects: the Gravity-Powered Boat with Electric Pump (page 36) and the Water Jet Boat (page 95). You can use the pump to add water to the reservoir that provides the power for the Gravity-Powered Boat. Or, you can use the pump to suck up water from your ocean and spit it out the back of the boat to drive it. The pump could be mounted on the back of the transom so you don't have to cut a hole in the hull. The pump will sit in the water, attached to the back of the boat, pumping water to the rear.

Science

An impeller is the rotating part of a centrifugal pump or turbine. It is encased in a housing and pushes water through pipes. A propeller is different; it usually is not encased in anything and pushes water in one direction to move a boat in the other direction. A propeller moves a vessel through water, and an impeller moves water through a vessel.

Siphon Pump

A *siphon* allows you to move liquids from a place of higher elevation to a place of lower elevation. You fill a tube with the liquid and block the ends so the liquid can't exit. Then put one end of the tube in the liquid at a higher elevation. When you allow the liquid to leave the tube at the lower end, it will flow.

As long as the lower end of the tube is at a lower elevation than the upper end, the flow will continue. Gravity pulls the liquid down the tube. The flow continues because any partial vacuum inside the tube will be filled by water pushed into the upper end. Air pressure at the upper end of the tube (atmospheric pressure) will be higher than pressure inside the tube and will push water into the upper end to keep the flow going.

Here is a pump that raises the pressure inside a closed container at the upper end of the tube to force water into the tube and out the other end. The source of the pressure is a bike pump, and the only trick to making this pump is getting the air from the pump into a closed container.

Materials

2-liter plastic soda bottle with cap
Drill and bits
Basketball inflating needle
Hot glue gun
Vinyl tubing, ¼-inch outside diameter
Water
Bicycle pump

Build It

1. A 2-liter soda bottle is the container of choice due to its cost and availability. Drill two holes in the cap. The position of these holes is critical; if they are too close together you won't be able to mount the inflating needle and tube. It's easier to drill the holes from the inside of the cap. Drill a ¼-inch hole as close to the side of the cap as possible, without hitting the side. You will insert a vinyl tube with a ¼-inch outside diameter through this hole.

2. Drill a second hole on the opposite side, as close to the side of the cap as you can. This hole requires a ⁵⁄₆₄-inch drill bit. Into this hole, push an inflating needle for a basketball.

3. With the needle partially in its hole, cover the sides of the needle with hot glue and push the needle in as far as it will go. Hold it in place until the glue hardens.

4. Push the piece of ¼-inch outside diameter vinyl tubing through the other hole. Screw the cap onto the bottle so you can gauge how much tube should be pushed through the hole. The tube should reach to the bottom of the bottle. When you

have the right length of tube pushed through the hole, pull the hose out ½ inch, coat the tube all the way around with hot glue, and pull the hose back ½ inch so the glue is drawn into the hole in the cap.

5. To further ensure a good seal, turn the cap over and drop a big glob of molten glue into the inside of the cap around the vinyl tube and inflating needle.

Test It

To operate the pump, fill the bottle with water and screw on the cap. Connect a bicycle tire pump to the inflating needle. Pump away.

Science

The pump pushes air into the bottle, increasing the pressure. As long as the bottle is sealed, the increased pressure will force water up the vinyl tube and out.

5

Going Down: Submarines

Going beneath the water surface adds a third dimension of complexity that requires more control. You can make a submarine travel forward and backward using motors, like a boat, but how do you make it go up and down?

Start with some quick and simple projects and then move on to the much more complex and very cool remotely operated vehicle—the ROV.

Medusa Submarine

This submarine resembles a bell-shaped jellyfish called the *medusa*.

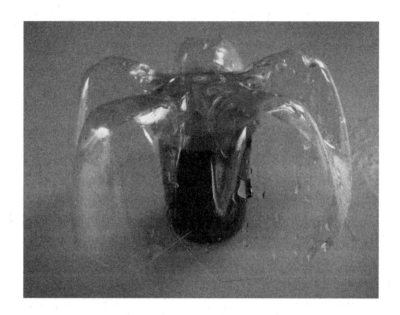

Adult supervision required

Materials

Scissors
2-liter plastic soda bottle
Film canister (35 mm), black
Hot glue gun

Drill and bits
10 pennies
Box of Alka-Seltzer tablets
(or generic equivalent)

Build It

1. Using scissors, cut off the bottom 2 inches of a 2-liter soda bottle. This bottom piece will be the hull of the submarine.
2. Take the lid from a black 35 mm film canister and hot glue it to the center of the soda bottle, on the inside. Why a black canister? Black film canisters have flat lids that make a better surface for gluing.
3. Drill two ⅛-inch-diameter holes in the side of the film canister. One hole should be ¼ inch above the bottom of the canister and the other hole about ¼ inch from the top. These holes allow water into the engine and let gas bubbles escape.

4. Drop 10 pennies into the canister. Add one Alka-Seltzer tablet on top of the pennies and push the canister onto its lid. The Medusa Submarine is ready.

Test It

Hold the Medusa Submarine underwater and tilt it to one side to let the air trapped under the submarine hull to escape. The Medusa Submarine should fall to the bottom of your ocean, but quickly return to the surface.

What's happening? Once wet, the Alka-Seltzer tablet fizzes. The water allows two dry ingredients—sodium bicarbonate and citric acid—in the tablet to react with each other to generate carbon dioxide gas. This gas rises to the top of the film canister, escapes through the tiny hole, and fills the Medusa hull with buoyancy-providing gas.

Once the Medusa Submarine is back on the surface, it will vent some of the trapped gas and be ready to dive again. Tipping it farther to one side will allow it to sink. Then the still-active tablet will bring it back to the surface. You have time for two or three dives before the tablet is shot.

Sailing Further

Try cutting a V-shaped notch in one side of the hull to help let gas escape. When you snap the film canister back into the lid, align the top hole in the film canister with this notch as the gas builds up in the part of the hull next to the hole.

Or try using fewer pennies in the canister. You need only enough ballast to pull the Medusa Submarine to the bottom. Any additional ballast will slow the upward ascent.

Science

Jellyfish, along with corals and anemones, belong to an animal group whose members have stinging cells. The stinging cells are tiny arrows that fire when the cells contact something. The arrow lodges into its target and the cell pumps venom through a tube to the arrow and into its prey.

The jellies have bodies shaped like a bell with hair-like tentacles streaming beneath the bell. The bell with tentacles reminded someone of Medusa, the Greek mythological monster with a head surrounded by snakes.

Organic Submarine

How cool is this? You can make a submarine out of a carrot!

The Medusa Submarine (page 152) uses carbon dioxide bubbles released by a dissolving Alka-Seltzer tablet to lift it off the bottom. In this project, baking powder is used. It causes a similar chemical reaction: an acid reacts chemically with sodium bicarbonate to create carbon dioxide gas. Baking powder is used in baking "quick breads" to create air pockets in the dough. (The alternatives to baking with baking powder are to use yeast to generate the carbon dioxide or to have flat, unleavened bread.)

Adult supervision required

Materials

Drill and bits
Bag of baby carrots (eat the leftovers)
Dowel, 1 inch long, ¼-inch diameter
Baking powder
Knife to trim the carrot

Build It

1. The Organic Submarine works best in a smaller ocean: a sink or, better yet, a plastic storage container with clear sides. Put a few inches of water in the container or sink.

2. Drill a ¼-inch hole through the center of a baby carrot. Use a 1-inch-long piece of ¼-inch-diameter dowel for the sub's *conning tower*, the small structure that

rises above the deck of a submarine. Push the conning tower into the hole about halfway through the submarine.

3. Test the buoyancy of your organic submarine by throwing it into a container or sink of water. By throwing it in you ensure it will tumble and lose any air pockets in the hole below the conning tower. The sub should have slight *negative buoyancy*—that is, it should sink to the bottom, but very slowly. The wood conning tower will keep the submarine upright. If the sub is *too* negatively buoyant—if it sinks too quickly—you can either use a longer piece of dowel for the conning tower or cut off a bit of the bow and stern. And if the sub has *positive buoyancy* instead—if it rises back to the surface and floats there—use a smaller piece of dowel or a larger carrot.

Test It

After testing the buoyancy of the submarine, take it out of the water and pack baking powder into the empty hole below the conning tower.

Put the carrot back in the water, turning it sideways to get rid of any air bubbles in the hole. Once the sub is on the bottom of the container, stand by to watch. You will see bubbles forming. After a few seconds the submarine should rise to the surface and then tip to one side and dive back to the bottom. It can repeat this vertical motion four or five times.

Ship's Log

Plastic diving submarines used to be given away as a prize in cereal boxes. They were a big hit and helped sell a million boxes of cereal. After a few years' absence, they are back on the market, sold in science catalogs and toy stores. You can see original 1955 toy submarine patent online by searching for "patent number 2,712,710."

Waterproof a Motor

To make a motorized submarine, you first need to waterproof the motors. This process will not keep out the water if the motors are in water deeper than a few inches, but it will protect the motors for shallow operations.

Adult supervision required

Materials

Wax candle
Adult helper
Pot for melting wax
Pot for boiling water
Stove
Motor
Masking tape
Wire strippers

Electrical wire, 22 gauge
Soldering gun (optional)
Drill and bits
Block of wood
Sheet of newspaper
Film canister (35 mm)
Heavy work gloves
Propelle

Build It

1. To waterproof motors, surround them with candle wax. Start by melting the candle in a double boiler (with an adult's help). Put the candle in a pot that will be used only for melting wax and put that in a cooking pot with water. Turn on the heat. The wax will melt at about 100°F, well below the water's boiling point.

2. While the wax is heating, cover any holes in the motor to be waterproofed with tape. The tape will keep the molten wax from entering and gumming up the motor. There are holes on the motor housing, both front and back, and some motors have vents on the sides as well. Tiny pieces of masking tape will protect the motor.

3. Strip the insulation off two pieces of electrical wire. The pieces should be 12 to 18 inches long.

4. Feed one uninsulated end of the wire into the holes in the two electrical connections on the motor. Twist the wire ends around themselves to make good electrical connections and prevent them from slipping off. Soldering is not necessary but a good insurance. Solder melts at 190°F or higher, so the molten wax, which will be poured on top, will not melt it.

5. Make a stand to hold your motor(s) while the wax hardens. Drill one ⁵⁄₆₄-inch hole for each motor in a block of wood. Space the holes a couple of inches apart. Put the block with drilled holes on top of a sheet of newspaper so dripping wax doesn't get on the work surface.

6. Use the same drill bit to drill a hole in the bottom of a 35 mm film canister. The hole has to be in the center of the bottom. If the drill bit is long enough, drill it

from the inside of the canister. This will make it easier to push the motor shaft through the hole.

7. Slide the motor, now with its vent openings covered with tape and with wires connected to its terminals, into the film canister so the motor shaft sticks out through the hole.

8. With a heavy work glove on, hold the canister and pour wax into it. You don't need to fill the canister; just make sure the motor and terminals are covered.

9. Insert the motor shaft into one of the holes in the block of wood and let it cool for 10 minutes. When the wax has hardened, it will form a protective seal around the motor. Water can still get into the canister through the opening for the motor shaft, but not enough to do any harm.

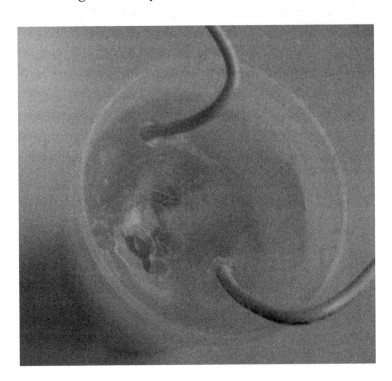

10. Push a propeller onto the motor shaft. The one shown below is a boat propeller from a science catalog, but you could use a different propeller or make one as described in the Motorboat project (page 78).

Sub Duck

With the waterproof motor you just made, you can make a Sub Duck. Although the duck rides on the surface, the motor is underwater.

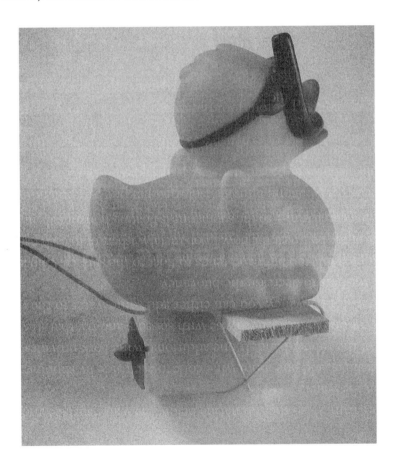

Materials

Coping saw
Wooden paint stirrer
Hot glue gun
Rubber duck, at least 3 inches wide and long
Waterproof motor and propeller (page 158)
2 rubber bands
2 AA batteries
Battery case for AA batteries
Pencil

Build It

1. To enable adjustments side to side, forward and back, don't glue the waterproof motor to the duck. Instead, use a coping saw to cut a piece of a wooden paint stirrer, and hot glue it to the bottom of the duck. The piece shown is just ¼ inch longer than the width of the base of the duck.
2. With the wood in place, attach the motor to it with two rubber bands looped over the ends of the paint stirrer.

Test It

Connect the ends of the two wires to a battery pack with two AA batteries. If the duck moves backward, reverse the connections to the battery pack.

On the first water test of the duck, the motor was off center, pulling the duck down to one side. That was easily corrected by sliding the motor under the rubber bands. Once the duck was on an even keel, the tests revealed a strong directional preference. This motor pushed much better than it pulled. That is, it moved the duck much faster when it was pushing water away from the film canister that held the motor than when it was pushing water toward the film canister. The propeller was smaller than the diameter of the film canister, so in the less effective direction it was pushing water directly onto the canister—similar to putting a fan on a boat to blow the sails. It resulted in lots of action, but not much motion.

Sailing Further

Once you are satisfied that the Sub Duck is working, use a pencil to trace the outline of the motor onto the paint stirrer. Remove the motor and dry both the wood and motor. Once the wood is completely dry, glue the motor to the stirrer on top of the traced outline. Press the motor firmly against the stirrer while the glue is drying. The glue will hold but will release later with a firm yank when you want to use the motor for another project.

Bathyscaphe

A *bathyscaphe is* a self-propelled submersible made for deep-sea diving. Building one is an opportunity to put that waterproof motor to work in a new direction: down. And up!

Adult supervision required

Materials

Pocketknife
Waterproof motor
Duct tape
2 film canisters (35 mm) with lids
2 AA batteries
Battery case for AA batteries
Metal washers or pennies (optional)
DPCO switch (optional)
Soldering gun (optional)
Adult helper (for optional steps)

Build It

1. This is a quick build. Use a pocketknife to cut a small notch in the lip of the waterproof motor housing as a port for the wires to exit.

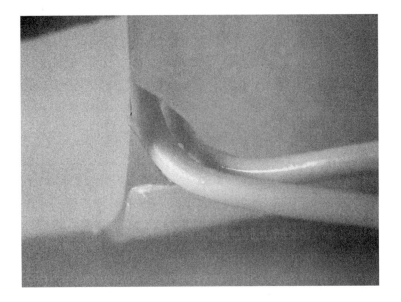

2. Feed the wires through the notch.

3. Tape a film canister on top of the waterproof motor. Position the film canister so its lid is up.

4. Before operating the motor, test the ballast. The bathyscaphe should be as close to *neutrally buoyant* as possible. That is, when placed in water it should float in the water column and rise and fall with just a gentle nudge. With an air-filled film canister the bathyscaphe will be too buoyant and will bob at the surface. Pop open the lid and add some water. Seal the canister and try it again. Keep adding water until it is neutrally buoyant. You could use metal washers or pennies instead

of water. If for some reason your waterproof motor is too heavy for the buoyancy provided by one film canister, add a second film canister on top.

Test It

Connect the motor wires to the leads from a battery pack with two AA batteries. The bathyscaphe will either move up or down. To go in the other direction, reverse the connection.

Sailing Further

Since switching the wires back and forth is a bother, you may want to wire in a DPCO (double-pole, center-off) switch, available at electronics supply stores. In one position the switch will drive the bathyscaphe up; in the center position, the motor will be off; and when the switch is thrown in the other direction, the sub will go down. The diagram below shows how to wire the switch; ask an adult helper to solder the connections if you will use the Bathyscaphe more than a few times. (For more details on how to wire a DPCO switch, see the Submersible ROV project, page 190.)

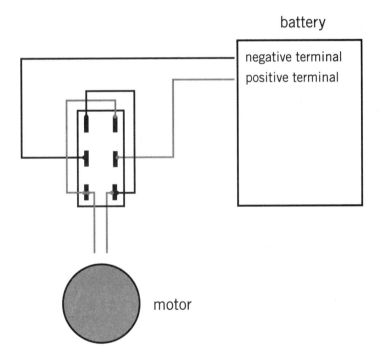

Ship's Log

The first humans to glimpse animals living in the deep sea were William Beebe and Otis Barton in the 1930s. They climbed into a steel sphere and were lowered to depths greater than a half mile. Their submersible was a *bathysphere*; *bathy* refers to depth and *sphere* describes the shape of the craft. A bathysphere is tethered to a cable held by a ship—unlike a bathyscaphe, which can move itself up and down.

August Piccard built the first bathyscaphe in the late 1940s. His son, Jacques Piccard, and US Navy Lt. Don Walsh dove in a second-generation bathyscaphe called the *Trieste* to set a world record for depth of 35,813 feet (10,916 m). They made this dive in the deepest known spot in the ocean, the Challenger Deep, so unless a new deepest spot is discovered their record will not be broken.

Electric Submarine

This model is self-contained—it carries its own batteries and can zip around underwater. The next project (page 176) shows how to waterproof the batteries. Or you can operate the Electric Submarine as a remotely operated vehicle (ROV) and keep the batteries out of the water.

Materials

Milk carton hull (page 10)
Scissors
Hot glue gun
Waterproof motor with propeller
Awl
Single hole punch
2 rubber bands

4 wine corks or film canisters (35 mm)
Waterproof battery case (see page 176)
3 large paper clips
Metal washers (small box)
2 alligator clip leads (optional)
Knife blade switch (optional)

Build It

1. Start with a milk carton hull, just like for the boats in previous projects. Cut off the transom, the back of the boat that was the bottom of the carton. Also cut away as much of the front of the hull as you can, leaving only the stem. These cuts remove parts of the hull that would add drag and slow down the submarine.

2. At the back of the hull, hot glue the waterproof motor to the underside of the hull. The propeller should face aft and the motor should be centered.

3. With an awl, poke a small hole in the center of the bottom of the hull, just forward of the motor, so the wires can pass through to the other side.

4. The motor is heavy and the milk carton hull doesn't provide much buoyancy, so you will need to add some buoyancy. With a single hole punch, punch two holes in both sides of the submarine. The holes will give you spots to attach buoyancy. Slide a rubber band through a hole on one side of the boat and loop each end around a wine cork or film canister. Attach a second cork or canister with a second rubber band on the other side of the submarine. If the buoyancy is too far forward or backward, you can move it by punching new holes in both sides and attaching the corks or film canisters at the new holes.

5. Test the buoyancy by placing the waterproof battery pack (see page 176) in the hull and securing it to one side of the hull with a large paper clip. The paper clip keeps the neutrally buoyant battery pack from sliding around and disrupting the

submarine's trim. Push the submarine below the water surface and watch how it balances in the water.

6. If the back sinks, add one more wine cork to each side by slipping each one into the loops of the rubber band. If one additional wine cork provides too much buoyancy, cut one in half lengthwise with scissors and try that. If you are using film canisters for buoyancy, you can either add some water to the canister or add a few metal washers to decrease the buoyancy.

7. The bow is probably too light and tends to float to the surface. Clip a large paper clip to each side of the hull, near the bow. Loop metal washers onto each paper clip to get the submarine in neutral trim—so the submarine is floating horizontally in the water column.

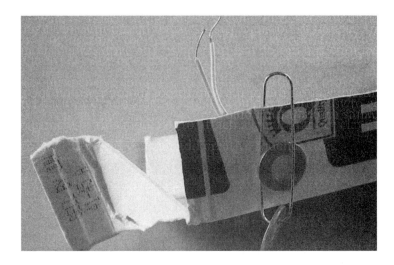

Test It

Connect the wires from the battery pack to the wires from the motor. Make the connections by holding two wires between each thumb and forefinger to see which way the boat moves. If it moves backward, switch the connections—that is, connect the red wire from the battery pack to the other wire from the motor, and the black wire from the battery pack to the motor wire previously connected to the red battery wire.

Either twist each pair of two bare wires together or use alligator clip leads to make the connections.

Sailing Further

For extended use, add a knife blade switch to the circuit. Twist the black battery pack wire together with its partner wire from the motor. Screw the red wire from the battery pack to one of the terminals on the knife blade switch and the remaining motor wire to the other terminal on the switch. Now you can control the motor just by opening and closing the switch.

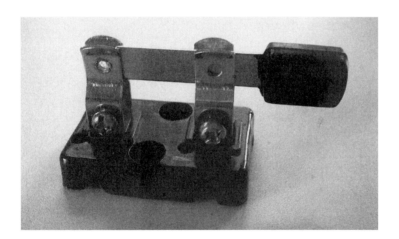

Science

The first submarines were powered by oars or by a propeller on a shaft that was rotated by hand. Today most submarines are propelled by electric motors powered by batteries. Either diesel engines or nuclear reactors with steam turbines are used to recharge the batteries.

Waterproof a Battery Case

Any container that goes underwater will eventually leak, and this battery case is no exception. But for use in shallow water, it can work well. If batteries do get wet, remove them from the case and dry them. They will probably continue to work.

Adult supervision required

Materials

Sealable plastic bag, snack size
2 AA batteries (alkaline batteries only) in battery pack
Hot glue gun (low temperature)
Duct tape (optional)

Build It

1. Place the battery pack and batteries in the small plastic bag. The wires from the battery pack should exit the bag opening at one end. Seal the bag shut. If you push the two bag halves together firmly enough, the seal will withstand modest water depths, except at the end where the wires protrude. Before sealing that end, make sure all the air is out of the bag.
2. Lower the bag in a sink or bucket of water up to the level of the seal. The water pressure will push out all the air and, as you remove the bag, little air will sneak back in.
3. Separate the top edges of the two sides of the bag where the wires come out. Into this tiny area, put in one small drop of hot glue. The glue will melt the plastic it touches and surround the wires with a molten stew of hot glue and plastic. When the glue and plastic solidify, they will make a good seal. I also added a bit of duct tape.

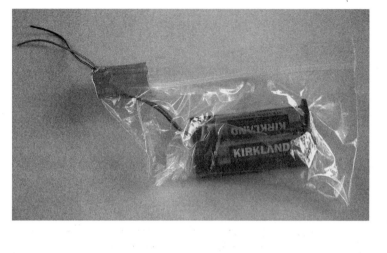

Sailing Further

What happens when the batteries die and need to be replaced? Open the waterproof bag starting at the end opposite to where the wires are. Pull out the battery case, being careful not to break the seal around the wires. Change the batteries in the case. Once the new batteries are in the battery pack, push it back in the bag, remove the air as before, and seal the bag.

Science

A dry-cell battery getting wet is not a problem. Remove it from the water and dry it off. But it's a bad idea to leave a battery in water, as with time the battery will short circuit and its case will corrode.

Check to see that your waterproof bag doesn't have water inside it after it has been underwater. If it does, open the bag away from the wire seal, take the batteries out of the pack, and dry them with a paper towel. Let the battery pack dry before reusing it.

Submersible ROV

An *ROV* is a remotely operated vehicle. It gets its electrical power and is controlled from the surface. ROVs were first used in the late 1950s and have become important tools in marine science and engineering. They can search for shipwrecks at depths far deeper than divers can go and aren't as risky or expensive as using a submersible with human crew.

This model uses inexpensive components that can control its movements up and down, forward and backward, and side to side. It would be fairly easy to add a small underwater video camera to this model or to attach a small grabber claw. You will learn how to build the basic ROV, and you can add creative touches later.

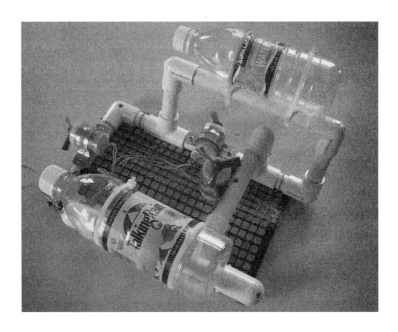

The overall design is modified from the Seaperch project described in the book *Build Your Own Underwater Robot and Other Wet Projects* by Harry Bohm. It uses PVC pipes for the body, empty 1-liter soda bottles for buoyancy, and three waterproof motors for propulsion. Electrical power is provided from the surface, and controls for each motor are mounted in a small plastic box. Once the Submersible ROV is built and balanced underwater, it moves smartly in response to the operator's controls.

Adult supervision required

Materials

PVC pipe, ½-inch diameter, 60 inches

Hacksaw or PVC pipe cutter

Adult helper

Drill and bits

10 PVC elbows

4 PVC T-joints

Heavy scissors

Plastic netting (from a produce bag or plastic fence)

Plastic cable ties (or small pieces of wire)

Metal weights: nuts, bolts, nails, washers

2 1-liter plastic water bottles with caps

3 waterproof motors

2 9-volt batteries

Duct tape

3 hose or pipe clamps to hold motors

Marking pen

Screws, ½ inch long, panhead metal

Electrical wire, 22 or 24 gauge

Wire strippers

Soldering gun

Electrical tape

Electrical project box (plastic)

3 DPCO switches

2 alligator clip leads

Voltmeter (optional)

Build It

Specific directions are listed on the following pages, but here are some general guidelines:

You will need 18 pieces of ½-inch PVC pipe (total length 51 inches). An easy way to cut the pipe is with a PVC ratchet cutter sold at hardware stores. The alternative is to use a hacksaw. Ask an adult to do the sawing.

There is no need to glue the PVC together. Even without glue the ROV will be robust.

The PVC frame has to allow any air inside the pipes to escape so that the buoyancy can be controlled. If you don't vent the air, water will slowly seep in and change the buoyancy of the ROV while you are operating it. To provide vents, as you're building this model, drill ¼-inch holes at various points in the PVC frame.

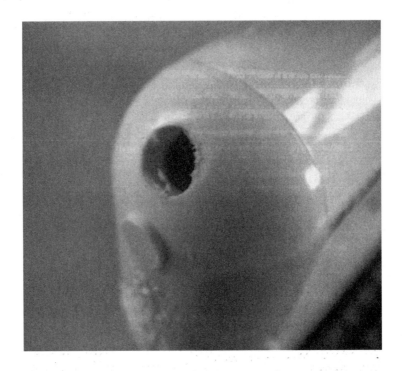

One more thing to be aware of: The ROV is an energy hog. It will quickly drain batteries.

Now it's time to build.

1. Make two cross pieces. One of these forms the stern of the ROV and the other is the forward cross brace. Each one holds a motor. Each assembly uses three pieces of PVC: one that is 4½ inches long and two pieces that are 1½ inches

long, plus two PVC elbows. Assemble the two pieces, drill air vent holes, and set them aside.

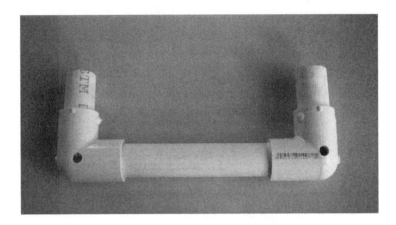

2. Make two pieces for the upper frames, one for each side of the ROV. The longer PVC piece for each is 6½ inches long. The two shorter pieces for each side are 3 inches long. Assemble each side with two elbow joints. Drill air vent holes and set them aside.

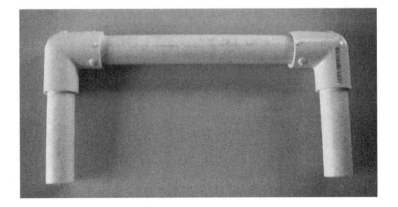

3. Make the lower frame for each side. Connect two T-joints with a 4-inch piece of PVC. Add a 1½-inch piece of PVC to one of the T-joints on each side. To this short section of pipe, connect an elbow joint on each side.

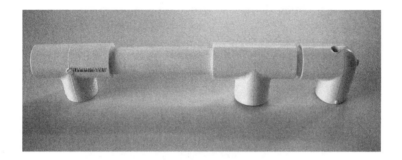

4. For each side, connect the upper frames (step 2) to the lower frames (step 3). Drill vent holes and set aside.

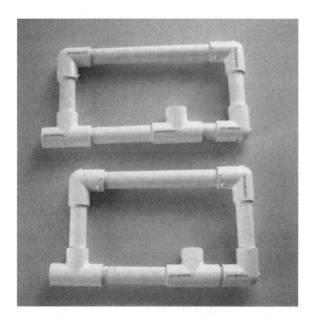

5. Complete the assembly of the ROV frame by connecting the stern and the forward cross brace (step 1) to the each side (step 4).

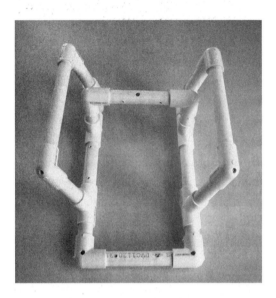

6. Attach the plastic netting. Cut a piece of plastic netting 7 inches by 12 inches. The netting can be any material that is light, strong, and open to water moving through it. An onion or citrus fruit plastic bag or plastic netting will work.

7. Set the netting down and place the ROV frame on top. Use either plastic cable ties or pieces of wire to hold the netting to the bottom of the frame.

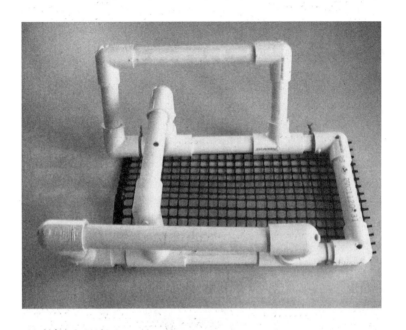

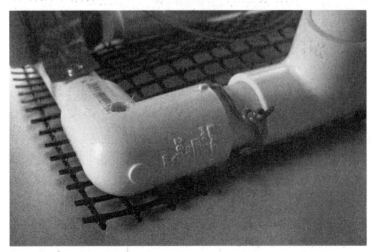

8. The ROV will work perfectly without the netting, but the netting makes it easier to adjust buoyancy. Rest a bolt or large nail on the netting to decrease the positive buoyancy or remove it to make the ROV less negatively buoyant.

9. Add the buoyancy chambers. Use two 1-liter water bottles with caps to provide buoyancy. Attach them to the upper arms of each side piece with two plastic cable ties.

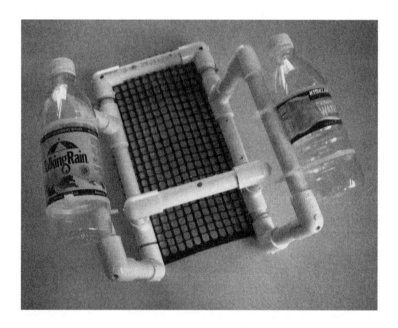

10. Make the waterproof motors. If you haven't waterproofed three motors for earlier projects, do so now. See instructions on page 158.

11. Test each motor to ensure that it works before going further. Connect the two

wires from the motor terminals to a 9-volt battery. If the motor doesn't work, you can try to repair it by removing the wax, but it is easier to replace the motor and waterproof it. Wrap each waterproofed motor with two windings of duct tape.

12. Mount the motors on the ROV frame. Use hose or pipe clamps to hold the waterproof motors in place. The motor that will drive the ROV forward and backward is mounted on the stern cross member, with the *propeller facing forward*. The motor that controls ascent and descent mounts on the forward cross brace, with the *propeller facing up*. The motor that moves the ROV left and right is mounted on one of the lower side frames, with the *propeller facing outward*. Use the hose clamp and a marking pen to mark where holes for screws should be

drilled. Drill the holes (sized for the screws you have), position each clamp, and insert screws into the holes—but do not tighten them yet.

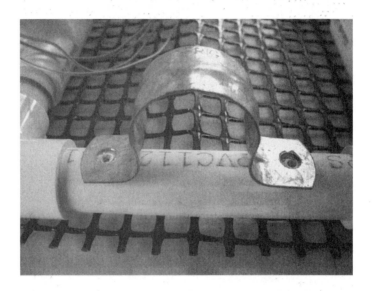

13. Insert a waterproof motor under each clamp, then tighten the screws.

14. All that remains is providing power to the motors. Estimate how deep you will drive your ROV and cut six pieces of wire that distance, plus 30 percent. Strip the insulation off each end of the six wires.

15. Twist the uninsulated end of each wire you just cut around the uninsulated end of each wire coming from a motor. Ask an adult to solder each connection and wrap each with electrical tape.

16. Mark the other end of each wire with a piece of tape and writing to remind you which pair of wires goes to each motor. Then use tape or cable ties every two feet to bind the six wires together.

17. Test the connections by touching the two wires for each motor to a battery or battery pack. If they all work, you are ready to launch.

18. You can operate the ROV by touching the wires from the ROV to a battery. However, the operation will be easier and more fun if you wire switches to control each motor. Electronic stores sell plastic project boxes into which you can mount switches. The smallest box to get is 4 inches by 2 inches by 1 inch.

Alternatively, you could use a much large plastic box: either a food storage container or a plastic lunch box.

19. Cut two more pieces of wire about 3 feet long, and strip the insulation from each end. These wires will come into the box carrying electrical power, one for the positive side and one for the negative side. They will connect to each of three switches to provide electricity to each motor. Operating each switch will drive its motor clockwise or counterclockwise, or will shut power off. Drill a small hole in the side of the box for these two wires to enter the box.

20. Mount three DPCO (double-pole, center-off) switches in the lid of the plastic box. Drill one hole for each. Size the holes to match the size of the base of the switch; the package the switches come in often specifies the size of the drill bit required. Insert a switch in each hole and secure it in place by screwing the nut onto the threaded base from the underside of the lid.

21. Cut six pieces of wire, each about 2 inches long, and strip the insulation from

the ends of each. Insert one wire into the hole in either of the center terminals of a switch, twist the wire around itself, and have an adult solder it. When you are finished, each switch should have two short wires soldered to its two center terminals. Connect one of these wires from each switch to one of the power-carrying wires; twist the uninsulated ends of all four wires together and have an adult solder them. Wrap with electrical tape.

22. Repeat with the other four wires—the remaining one from each switch and the second power-carrying wire. At this point you have connected electricity to each switch. Now you'll connect one motor to each switch.

23. Drill a hole in the side of the box so the six wires from the motors can fit through the hole. Push the two wires coming from one of the motors through a hole in the project box. Connect these two wires to the terminals at one end of the first switch. Slide the uninsulated end of each wire through a hole in a terminal, twist the wire onto itself, and solder. Repeat this for the other two switches. Now you can operate each motor in one direction and turn it off.

24. To be able to turn the motor in the other direction, you need to add six more wires. These wires will reverse the flow of electricity through each switch. Assume that the first switch is wired so the positive battery terminal is connected to the right center terminal of the first switch and that the negative battery terminal is connected to the left center terminal. With the switch in the center position, nothing happens. When you push the switch toward the end where the motor wires are connected, the motor will spin. To get the motor to spin in the opposite direction, you need to reverse the current flow to the motor. Now you want the *positive* battery wire (on the right side) connected to the motor wire that was connected to the *negative* battery wire. You can switch the connections by using a short piece of wire to connect the bottom left terminal to the top right terminal

on the switch and completing the circuit by connecting the bottom right terminal to the top left terminal. If that seems complicated, don't worry; the next two steps will tell you exactly what to do.

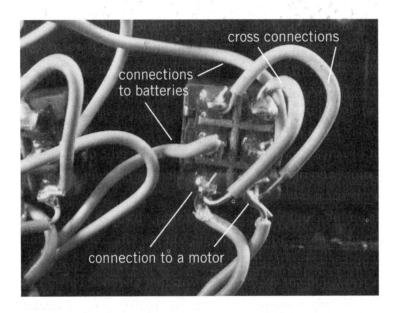

25. Cut six wires, each about 1½ inches long, and strip the ends off each. Take one wire and poke it through the hole in the terminal already occupied by one of the wires going to a motor. Twist the uninsulated end onto itself and have an adult solder it in place.
26. If this newly added wire is attached to the lower left terminal, connect its other end to the upper right terminal of the same switch. Take a second piece of the wire and connect the lower right terminal (already occupied by a wire going to a motor) to the upper left terminal.
27. Look at the switch. Power comes into the center terminals. If the switch is

pulled down, power goes to the motor. If the switch is in the center position, no power is provided. If the switch is pushed up, power again goes to the motor but the polarity is reversed (the electrons flow in the opposite direction), and the motor will rotate in the opposite direction. The short wires that connect opposite sides of the upper and lower terminals reverse which side of the motor receives positive and negative power. You will appreciate all this messy wiring when you are operating your ROV.

28. Put the lid back on the project box and screw it shut.

29. Connect the two power-carrying wires from the control box to a 9-volt battery. Test each of the switches to see that each motor spins, stops, and reverses direction depending on the position of the switch. If none of the motors spin, you either need more power or have a faulty connection. You can use a voltmeter to follow the voltage through the system to see where it stops, by touching the voltmeter probes to the positive and negative wires everywhere they connect to a different part of the system. But first, see if the circuits just need more power.

30. Replace the single battery with two 9-volt batteries connected in parallel. Use one alligator clip lead to connect the positive terminals of each 9-volt battery. Use another clip lead to connect the negative terminals of the two batteries. If you are not sure which is positive and negative, look for small symbols on the sides of the battery case near the terminals. Connect one power-carrying wire from the project box to one of the positive terminals and the other wire to one of the negative terminals.

31. Test the ROV in water. First get it balanced fore and aft, side to side, and just slightly negatively buoyant. Add and move weights on the plastic netting to get the correct trim. Then try each of the switches.

32. In all the wiring, you have not paid attention to which way each motor drives the ROV. Now it is time to record what each position of the three switches does.

Put a piece of masking tape on the lid of the project box above and below each switch to record which switch controls which motor and which switch direction corresponds to which direction the ROV moves.

Test It

Operating the ROV is like driving a radio-controlled car, but much harder. Not only do you have to figure out how to control the craft as it changes its position relative to you, but you also have one more dimension of movement to control. If you operate it in a natural body of water, you will also have the natural motion of the water to contend with. Have fun!

6

Projects for a Tiny Sea

Here are some experiments to run and demonstrations to do to amaze your friends. They require only a little water and a few materials.

Amazing Holdup

Even if you've seen this before, you expect the water in the photo below to fall from the glass. Of course, if you don't do it right, the water will fall. So here's how to do it (almost always) perfectly.

When doing this the first time, try it over a sink or outside where a mistake won't be quite as painful to clean up. But after you've gained confidence you can perform this without a net, or sink.

Materials

Drinking glass, 6- to 12-ounce
Water
Scissors

Cereal box
Mop (just in case)

Build It

1. Pick a glass, any glass, and fill it halfway with water.
2. Cut a circle or square a bit larger than the diameter of the glass out of a cereal box. Put this piece on top of the glass with the (unprinted) inside of the box facing the water. The printing on the other side of the box can prevent the cardboard from making a good seal with the rim of the glass, so keep the printed side up.
3. Turn the glass over while holding the cardboard to the rim of the glass. Hold it there for a few seconds to let the cardboard get wet and to build the anticipation in your audience.
4. Now, pull your hand away and—voilà!—the water stays in the glass.

Going Further

When you squeeze the cardboard against the rim of the glass, you squeeze a bit of air from the glass. When you release your grip, the pressure inside the glass decreases just a bit. It is now at lower pressure than the air pressure outside the glass. Atmospheric pressure pushes the cardboard up against the rim of the glass with greater force than the force of gravity pulling the water down.

We forget that we live in a column of air that stretches some 60 miles from the Earth's surface upward. Although air is very light, 60 miles of air piled up does have weight, about 14 pounds per square inch. If you look at the glass you used, its surface area is probably about 7 square inches (1.5-inch radius squared, multiplied by pi, 3.14), so the force holding the cardboard against the glass is 98 pounds (assuming a complete vacuum inside the glass, which is not true). If the pressure inside the glass were zero, the cardboard would be sucked in and the seal would be broken. But you didn't remove much air, so the pressure inside was not much less than 14 pounds per square inch. It was just enough to hold up the water.

Science

It takes 60 miles of air piled on top of air to weigh the same as 33 feet of water. The weight of a column of air 60 miles tall is the same as that of a column of water 33 feet tall. Riding in a car up a mountain pass you may gain 1,000 feet of elevation before your ears pop to relieve the pressure. But dive to the bottom of a swimming pool and you'll feel the pressure on your eardrums in just a few feet.

Mustard Submarine

This is a fun way to see the effects of pressure on buoyancy. If performed with a bit of showmanship, this exercise can excite a whole crowd of onlookers.

Materials

Mustard or ketchup packet
Paper clips
Wire cutters
Water
2-liter plastic soda bottle with cap

Build It

1. To prepare for this demonstration, balance a mustard or ketchup packet in the water so that it is just slightly buoyant. You do this by clipping a paper clip to one end of the packet. If packet and paper clip immediately bob back to the surface after you push them underwater, add a second paper clip or just half a paper clip (cut it with wire cutters) to reduce the buoyancy.
2. When you have the packet weighted so that it just barely floats with the weight, squeeze it into an empty 2-liter soda bottle.

3. Fill the bottle *all the way to the rim* with water—no air—and screw on the cap. You don't want to have any air at the top of the bottle, as this will give away the secret to the demonstration.

Test It

Squeeze the bottle. The Mustard Submarine sinks to the bottom of the bottle. Release your grip and it rises to the top. So what is the magic in the mustard?

When you squeeze the bottle you increase the pressure inside. If there is any air inside the bottle, the air will compress and you will bend the side of the bottle as you squeeze it, and your audience will figure out the trick. The volume of air will be reduced as the pressure increases. Air is a compressible fluid. Water, however, is not very compressible. If the bottle is full of water, even though you've increased the pressure inside, the volume of water remains nearly the same. There would be no noticeable change in the bottle as you squeeze.

What's happening inside the mustard packet? Although the packet is nearly filled with liquid mustard, there is a small pocket of air inside. The volume of this air decreases as the pressure inside the bottle increases. With the air taking up less volume, it provides less buoyancy to the packet, so the packet falls. Release your grip slightly and the pressure inside the bottle and packet is reduced, the volume of air inside the packet increases, the buoyancy increases, and the packet floats to the top.

Going Further

When doing this with others, have someone stand beside you and hold out his hand, level with and next to the Mustard Submarine. Ask him to slowly lower his hand to the bottom of the bottle. As he does, squeeze the bottle so the submarine follows his hand. Tell him that he must really like mustard for the Mustard Submarine to follow him. Do this two or three times to focus your audience. Then dismiss your mustard-loving volunteer.

Hold the bottle in one hand and explain that the submarine moves only if someone who loves mustard stands beside it. Then, as you look off to the left and hold the bottle to the right, squeeze the bottle. Someone will tell you that the mustard packet is falling, but before you look at the bottle, release your grip while explaining again that it can't fall unless a mustard lover is pulling it down. By the time you look over at the bottle, the packet is again at the top and you can insist that the mustard hasn't moved. Again look away while squeezing the bottle, and look back only after you've released your grip and the packet has had time to rise. By the third time, your audience will be shouting at you to look at the bottle when the mustard packet is at the bottom.

At this point your personal safety will be at risk if you don't explain what is happening. Isn't it great to have eager learners!

Science

Most fish (96 percent of them) have sacs filled with air to help them maintain buoyancy for the depth they want. Their bodies can pump in or remove gas to change depths, like the Mustard Submarine. These air sacs are called swim bladders.

Foghorn

What would a nautical experience be without a foghorn? Here is a simple device that will knock seagulls off the lighthouse.

Materials

Tube, stiff cardboard or PVC
Scissors (for cardboard tube) or
    hacksaw (for PVC)
Sandpaper
Balloon
Drinking straw, milkshake or fat
Duct tape
Rubber band (optional)

Build It

1. Start with a stiff cardboard tube. A mailing tube will work, but the tube from a roll of paper towels isn't strong enough. PVC pipe works wonderfully; any size will work, but ¾ inch is ideal. Cut a piece about 6 inches long and sand down the edges.
2. Cut the mouth off a latex balloon. Don't discard the mouth; you can use it as a one-way valve for a pump (see the Diaphragm Pump project, page 138). At the other end of the balloon, farthest away from the mouth, nip off the very end. You want this cut to be small, just large enough so you can slide a milkshake or fat drinking straw through the hole, which is the next step.

3. Slide the straw into the balloon and out the hole you just cut. Let ½ inch of the straw protrude through the opening, with the rest of the straw inside the balloon.

4. Secure the edge of the hole in the balloon to the straw. A tiny strip of duct tape works best. Turn the balloon inside out so the taped joint you just made is now on the *inside* of the balloon. Then pull the balloon onto the tube.

5. Pull the sides of the balloon down onto the tube so the tube opening is covered by a nearly flat section of the balloon, with the straw protruding from the center. Now is the time to test your foghorn. See any fog?

Test It

Grab the pipe with one hand holding the balloon to make sure no air can escape between the balloon and the sides of the pipe. Pull the straw lightly to one side and down.

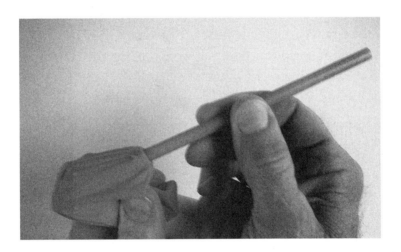

Put your lips on the straw and blow hard. If no sounds emerge, pull the straw more strongly to the side and blow again. You should see seagulls shaking their heads, wondering what that sound was.

Going Further

As air travels the length of the straw, it slows down due to drag on the walls of the straw. Reduce the drag to get faster moving air and louder sounds. To reduce the drag, cut the straw shorter.

If you bought an 8-foot length of PVC to make this foghorn, try playing the remaining 7 feet, 6 inches piece of pipe. Slide the balloon off the short section of PVC onto the longer piece. What difference in sound do you hear?

Find other size pipes and tubes to play. When you have one working well—by now the seagulls have flown away—use a rubber band or tape to secure the edges of the balloon onto the pipe.

Science

As you blew into the straw, the pressure inside the balloon rose. You were pushing air into the balloon, but it couldn't escape because you were holding the balloon down against the side of the tube. As pressure increased inside the end of the balloon, it stretched the balloon upward, away from the tube, allowing air to escape into the PVC tube.

When the air escaped, the pressure in the balloon dropped. With no pressure, the balloon contracted and closed the opening to the tube. But you were still blowing, so the balloon opened and closed again many times in a few seconds. The high-speed opening and closing of the balloon valve created the sound you heard. Watch the balloon while you blow to see it flutter as it expands and contracts to make the sound.

Make Steel Float

You know that steel won't float, right? That is correct, but you can get steel to stay on the surface of the water.

A ship is a big piece of steel, with a lot of other stuff thrown inside it, and it floats. But a ship is really just a rigid bag that keeps the water out of a large hole in the ocean. Because the hole is filled mostly with air, and because air weighs about 0.1 percent of the weight of the same volume of seawater, the ship is lighter than an equal volume of seawater. Let some water into the ship, like the *Titanic*, and down it goes. A steel ship filled with water doesn't float.

But there is another way to get steel to float or at least stay on the surface of water. The trick is to use a small piece of steel. You could use, for example, a paper clip.

Materials

2 large paper clips
Bowl
Water
Liquid soap

Build It

1. Rest a large paper clip onto the surface of a bowl filled with water *without touching the water*. An easy way to do this is to bend a second paper clip to make a handle

to hold and lower the first paper clip. Using this handle keeps your fingers from touching the water.

2. Once you rest the paper clip on the surface, pull the handle away and leave the paper clip resting on the surface.

Going Further

If your friends think this is cool, challenge them to try it. Tell them that only you can rest the paper clip on the water. While one of your friends is picking up the paper clip with the handle, quietly put a dab of liquid soap on one of your fingertips. Move the bowl to position it for your friend, and while moving it, touch the water surface with the same fingertip. When your friend tries to set the paper clip on the water, it will fall to the bottom.

If your friends challenge you to repeat your earlier success, throw out the water, rinse the bowl, and then refill it. The paper clip will float again.

Science

Many forces in nature don't "scale up." Surface tension is one. It works on a small scale, and because of this we often overlook its effects. The paper clip wasn't displacing water to float. Instead, water molecules at the surface were adhering so strongly to each other that they created a surface that supported the paper clip.

Water is a polar molecule. It has a positive side and a negative side, and like tiny magnets the water molecules stick to one another with much force—not enough force to hold up an aircraft carrier, but enough force to hold up a paper clip.

Adding soap separates the water molecules, reducing the surface tension, and letting the paper clip fall. You can't blow big bubbles in plain, nonsoapy water because the molecules hold onto each other too tightly. By adding soap you reduce the surface tension and allow the surface to stretch as you blow air into it.

Water is a strange, unique fluid that has amazing properties, surface tension being one of them. Many of the special properties of water are due to the alignment of the atoms in each molecule. You might suppose that the two hydrogen atoms in a water molecule would arrange themselves symmetrically around the oxygen atom, but they don't. The hydrogen atoms are drawn toward each other, due to a phenomenon called hydrogen bonding, so instead of being 180 degrees apart, they are about 105 degrees apart. Because of this asymmetric geometry, a water molecule ends up acting like a magnet, with a positive side where the two hydrogen atoms are and a negative side on the other end. Like magnets, water molecules stick to one another, which gives water its strong surface tension.

Make Some Waves

Internal waves, that is. Waves occur where the atmosphere meets the ocean's surface and underwater at the intersection of water layers that have different densities. These latter waves are internal to the water column, so they are called internal waves. The speed at which the waves move depends on the density difference between the two layers. If the layers have very different densities, the waves move faster.

This supposes that the less dense water is on top. If it isn't, the water column is unstable and will turn over with little or no external motion. Lakes in the fall cool at the surface as winter approaches. The upper layers become colder and hence denser, and sink to the bottom. As they do, they take along a new supply of oxygen (they gained from contact with the atmosphere at the surface) to replenish the oxygen levels exhausted over the summer months by animal respiration.

As long as the layer on top is less dense, it will tend to stay there. A passing internal wave will move the water up and down, but probably not mix the waters above with the water below.

Materials

2-liter plastic soda bottle with cap
Water
Food coloring
Vegetable oil

Build It

1. To make some waves, put two immiscible fluids into a 2-liter plastic bottle. *Immiscible* means the fluids don't mix, like oil and water. Fill the bottle halfway with water and add seven drops of food coloring. Give the bottle a good shake.
2. Fill up the bottle with a cheap vegetable oil and cap the bottle.

3. Lay the bottle on its side and watch the waves form, rebound off the end, and then die. In the ocean the waves keep going and going until they slam into a beach or cliff, but here you see them for only a few seconds.

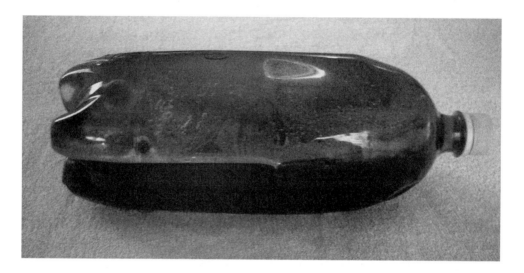

Science

Internal waves are responsible for the phenomenon known as dead water. Fridtjof Nansen, an Arctic explorer and Nobel Laureate, was the first to describe this phenomenon. A ship with its propeller at the depth where two layers of water intersect can find itself nearly stalled in this water. Instead of pushing the boat forward, the propeller creates internal waves, like the ones in the 2-liter bottle. Potential locations for dead water are in estuaries where fresh river water overrides the salty sea water.

Make Some More Waves

The wave machine used two fluids that don't mix, known as immiscible fluids. Even if you disturb them or mix them, they will separate. But what happens if you have two layers of the same fluid, like in an ocean or lake? The sun warms the upper layers, making them less dense. Rivers emptying into the ocean flood the ocean surface with fresh water, which is less dense.

What happens when two layers of the same fluid, one warm and fresh and the other cold and salty, are allowed to mix?

Materials

Salt
Water
Clear glass baking dish
Food coloring
Wax paper

Build It

1. To simulate the saltiness of seawater, add one cup of salt to two gallons of water. Place it into the refrigerator and allow it to get very cold.
2. Once it is very cold, pour the salty water into a clear glass baking dish, filling the dish halfway.
3. Make some colorful, warm fresh water to go on top. Use hot tap water and mix in a generous dose of food coloring. Stir well.

4. If you just pour the less-dense warm water into the dish, the two waters will mix—the downward momentum of the poured water will carry it to the bottom, across the bottom, and throughout the dish. In seconds the entire ocean will be colored. So to reduce the mixing, first lay a piece of wax paper cut to the size of the dish on top of the cold, salty water.

5. Now, carefully pour the second layer (warm water) onto the wax paper. Where the water spills over the edges of the paper it will drop into the salty layer and mix a bit, but not so much that it mixes the two layers.
6. Carefully pull out the wax paper to retain the two layers.

Science

With time, heat will conduct downward (and from the sides and bottom of the dish), reducing the temperature difference between the two fluids. Slowly, little pockets of salt water will mix with the fresh water, reducing the difference in salinity (the amount of salt in water). Gradually the entire dish will show a diluted shade of the color you added to the warm layer. Stirring by hand or with a waterproof motor (page 158) will mix the two fluids in seconds.

References

Bohm, Harry and Vickie Jensen. *Build Your Own Underwater Robot and Other Wet Projects.* Vancouver: Westcoast Words, 1997.

Sobey, Ed. *Unscrewed: Salvage and Reuse Motors, Gears, Switches, and More from Your Old Electronics.* Chicago: Chicago Review Press, 2011.

Sobey, Ed. *The Way Kitchens Work.* Chicago: Chicago Review Press, 2010.

Sobey, Ed, and Woody Sobey. *The Way Toys Work.* Chicago: Chicago Review Press, 2008.

Walker, Jearl. *The Flying Circus of Physics.* New York: John Wiley & Sons, 1977.

Appendix A

Sources for Materials

alligator clip leads: Electronics stores and science catalogs sell these. Get the shortest length possible and the cheapest ones; a small number of them will not work or will break quickly, but you still save money by not getting the more expensive ones.

aluminum roasting pans for extruded aluminum boats: Disposable aluminum pans are sold at grocery stores and restaurant supply stores.

balloons: Get 12-inch latex balloons at party stores.

DPCO switches: Double-pole, center-off switches are available at electronics supply stores.

fat straws: Fat straws or milkshake straws are available at fast-food restaurants. You can also purchase boxes of larger quantities at restaurant supply stores. For most applications, the shorter straws are preferable.

film canisters: Yes, people still take photographs on film, and some stores still process it, so you can get canisters at those places. Costco, for instance, gives them away. Also, enterprising people are selling this once-expendable, now-valuable item online.

gears: You can purchase small gears online through science stores such as Kelvin.com.

grid wall: When stores go out of business or remodel, they often get rid of the old grid wall from their display racks. It also can be purchased from vendors that sell store fixtures.

motors: Motors used to spin propellers in air need to rotate fast, more than 10,000 rpm. Cheap toy motors will work. These usually are rated for 3 to 6 volts of DC (battery) power. Generally they are forgiving, can be powered by 9-volt batteries, and can take a dunking in fresh water. When they have spun for the last time, they are easy to take apart to see how they work. Kelvin.com is the best source for cheap motors. Motors to use with paddleboats or in-water propellers should spin at slower rates. You can use the cheaper fast motors but will have better success with the more expensive and slower motors. Kelvin.com sells these as "solar motors." Solorbotics.com, Jameco.com, and American Science and Surplus (www.sciplus.com) are a few of the other companies that sell motors online. These companies call them gear motors, solar motors, and project motors. Check the motor shaft diameter to see if it will fit the propellers, pulleys, and gears you are purchasing.

nose hooks: These are used to power balsa airplanes powered by twisted rubber bands. Science supply catalogs are the best place to find them. You can purchase the entire plane and take off the nose hook, or look for a vendor that sells bags of just nose hooks.

paint stirrers: These are a great material for building. Paint stores and hardware stores give them away, but it would be nice to purchase something while you are there. If you need a lot of them, purchase them by the thousand online. For a few pennies more you can have the name of your organization printed on each one.

propellers: Science catalogs are the place to look. Hobby stores have a good supply, but theirs are too large to fit electric motors. Kelvin.com has several that fit on the shafts of motors the company sells.

pulleys: Small pulleys are available online at science stores such as Kelvin.com.

pumps: Pumps are more difficult to find. Some science supply catalogs carry them, but their inventory varies from time to time so you have to search. Harbor Freight (www.harborfreight.com) carries inexpensive solar-powered pumps for mini fountains. You can take these apart to get the pump. Considering that you are getting both a decent solar cell and a pump, this is a good deal.

solar cells: To power a motor, a solar cell has to output a voltage greater than the voltage the motor requires. Solar motors use low voltages, about 2 volts. If a solar cell outputs less than this, you need to have several cells to connect in series. By making the connection in series you add the output voltages of each cell. Two 1-volt output solar cells connected in series output a combined 2 volts (provided the sun is shining and they are facing the sun). Other motors may require higher current than is output by a single solar cell, in which case you can connect two cells in parallel. A parallel circuit connects the two positive terminals of two solar cells and connects the two negative terminals on each cell. A connection from the positive side goes to the motor, and one from the negative side goes to the other motor terminal. It can be difficult to determine how best to connect the cells (series or parallel), so try each approach connected to a motor to see which spins the motor fastest. Electronics stores online and science supply stores carry solar cells. Look first at Kelvin.com and Solarbotics.com.

steam engines: Most online retailers want to sell you the finished boat. Science stores like Kelvin.com will sell you just the engines.

supercapacitors: Online electronics stores and some science catalogs have these. Kelvin.com and Sparkfun.com carry them.

Appendix B
Meeting Science Standards

I don't claim that everyone who builds the models in this book will ace the science exams. But I do believe that they will understand science and technology much better than a learner who just listens to lectures or reads the text. With some direct instruction at a teachable moment, the model maker can both understand the science and pass the exam.

Here are the science standards included in making these models:

buoyancy and density: This is one of the many topics in physical science that is learned best by messing around with models. Listening to lectures is less effective and much less engaging than building an aluminum foil boat or getting an ROV to stay on an even keel. Build the model first and talk about the science later. The experiments in chapter 6 (page 195) provide opportunities for doing hands-on research on density, and boat and submarine projects provide opportunities for learning buoyancy.

chemical reaction: The Medusa Submarine and Organic Submarine use chemical reactions to generate carbon dioxide. The important point to understand is what a chemical reaction is and how it is different from a physical reaction. These two submarine projects open up the subject for discussion.

design and systems: Some school districts include design within science standards and others include it in engineering or technology standards. In either case, building the models in this book is an exercise in understanding design, making changes to improve the design, and using critical thinking.

electric circuits: All of the models in the Electric Boats section (page 60) require building circuits. In doing so, the learner becomes aware that switching connections to the battery causes the motor to spin in opposite directions. And, to get the motor to spin at all, the circuit has to be complete. To extend these activities, introduce voltmeters (available for a few dollars or less at online science stores) and have learners measure voltage, current, and resistance. Introduce Ohm's Law. Have them compare speed of movement at different voltages (combinations of different numbers of AA batteries). This could lead to graphing exercises, comparing voltages input or measured to speed of boats measured. Encourage learners to include switches and second motors in models so that they have to figure out how to wire them. Challenge them to see if series or parallel circuits work best.

energy and energy transformations: Propelling boats and submarines is about using energy stored in air pressure, water pressure, rubber bands, latent heat, or batteries, and transforming that energy into other forms to move. A typical scenario is starting with chemical energy in a battery, transforming that to mechanical energy (in a motor), and transforming the spinning motion to forward propulsion (with a propeller).

forces and motion: Nearly every activity in this book uses forces to cause motion. Propellers pushing water or air in one direction to move the boat or submarine in the opposite direction scream Newton's Third Law. You can work the other laws of motion into a discussion of what happened in these experiments.

gravity: This topic ties in nicely with buoyancy and with propulsion by water pressure in the Gravity-Powered Boat projects (pages 33 and 36).

hydraulics: This subject is omitted from science standards except in the context of erosion. A logical extension of using the boat models or pumps would be to try some hydraulic mining (erosion) on a clump of dirt or create riverbeds on a table of sand. Pump the water up with a pump or use water pistols to knock down the dirt.

investigations and experiments: Model builders are problem solvers on a quest to make something work. They are investigating, asking new questions, and conducting experiments continuously. The value in making the models is not just to create the completed model itself but to figure out how to solve each problem along the way and, in that process, learn. Watch kids work on these models. You will see their minds racing ahead, getting new ideas and trying new things. They are learning through experimenting, and the learning is occurring as fast as the human mind can operate.

measurement: Opportunities abound for measuring models and their performance. How many windings of a rubber band are required to move a boat 3 feet? Collect and graph data on the speed of an electric boat for various voltages (combinations of batteries). How much water is needed to fill your ocean?

motors: These are not listed specifically in content standards but are included in machines, the designed world, tools, and other topics. Empowering people to use motors gives them the freedom to explore, investigate, build, and learn. Once they learn, they will want to do more and experiment more on their own. Messing with motors empowers people to learn.

nature of matter: Steamboats address this topic directly, as does experimenting with density currents in chapter 6 (pages 210 and 213).

process of science and engineering investigations: Start the learning by engaging students in design-and-build challenges rather than giving them lectures. Once they start the hands-on work, they are engaged in a continuous stream of experiments. They don't listen to a lecture on the process of science; they do science.

solar energy: Learners can measure the voltage output from solar cells before adding them to power their boats. They can test them indoors under a variety of lighting conditions and outdoors with and without cloud cover. Encourage them to use more than one solar cell and to consider how to wire it: series or parallel.

sound: The Foghorn activity in chapter 6 (page 203) is about making sound and understanding how sound is made. You see the balloon vibrating, you can feel the vibrations, and you hear the sounds. As you play with different size pipes you understand how the size of the instrument controls the pitch of the sound. Instant learning, no lecture.

use of tools and materials: Sadly, many people don't know how to use a screwdriver and are afraid of using a saw. They quickly learn new skills and understand properties of materials through the design/build process. Once they acquire this knowledge and these skills, they want to apply them to new projects.

Glossary of Nautical Terms

aft: Located toward the after, or back, part of a boat or ship.

"Ahoy!": A traditional greeting among sailors, usually shouted from afar. Alexander Graham Bell suggested it should also become the greeting used on his invention the telephone, but today most people say "Hello."

amidships: The center of a boat or ship in either direction; either halfway between the bow and the stern, or halfway between the port and starboard sides.

amphibious vehicle: A craft that can be driven both in the water and on land.

ballast: Weight stored in the bottom of a ship or boat to help keep it upright in the water.

bathyscaphe: A submarine-like diving vessel that can move itself up and down but has little or no ability to move in any other direction.

bathysphere: A spherical diving vessel that is raised and lowered in the water via a cable held by a ship, with no ability to move on its own.

bilge: The lowest space inside a ship.

boat: A small nautical vessel—small enough to be carried on a ship.

bow: The pointy end at the front of a ship or boat. If there is no pointy end—think of a rectangular barge—the bow is the end that pushes water out of the way while the vessel is moving.

buoyancy: An object's ability to float in water. If an object is *positively buoyant*, it will rise to the surface and stay there. If it's *negatively buoyant*, it will sink to the bottom. If it's *neutrally buoyant*, it will remain floating at the same level, without rising or falling.

catamaran: A boat or ship with two hulls joined together.

chandlery: A store that sells hardware for ships and boats, charts, and other nautical essentials.

conning tower: The small structure that rises above the deck of a submarine.

deck: The surface inside a boat or ship that you walk on.

fore: Located toward the forward, or front, part of a boat or ship.

free board: The distance from the top edge of a vessel's hull to the water. The higher the free board is, the better able the vessel is to keep out water from waves.

gudgeon: On a rudder, the cylindrical fitting that holds the pintle. The pintle rotates inside the gudgeon, allowing the rudder to rotate while holding it to the boat.

hull: The outer skin of a ship or boat—the structure that keeps the water out and holds everything else in.

keel: The central structure that runs along the very bottom of a boat or ship's hull from bow to stern. Built of a strong material, the keel supports the rest of the hull and helps the vessel move in a straight line.

larboard: An older name for the left side of a boat or ship when facing toward the bow; it's now more commonly called the *port* side.

leeboard: The fins mounted on the hull of a sailboat to keep it moving in a straight line.

mast: A spar, or pole, used to support sails. Usually made of aluminum or wood, the mast is the part that sticks up on a sailboat.

pintle: On a rudder, the pin that fits into the cylindrical gudgeon to hold the rudder in place while allowing it to turn.

port: The left side of a boat or ship when facing toward the bow.

ROV: "Remotely Operated Vehicle." An underwater ROV is controlled from a ship, to which it sends back video so it can be positioned to take photographs or collect samples.

rudder: The part of a boat or ship that provides the ability to steer. By turning a wheel or tiller connected to the rudder, the person steering the vessel can change direction. The rudder deflects water to one side, pushing the stern of the boat in the opposite direction.

scuba: From the abbreviation for "Self-Contained Underwater Breathing Apparatus," a device for providing air to divers. It consists of a metal tank holding air under high pressure and a series of valves that reduce the pressure to deliver the air to the diver as he or she needs it.

semisubmersible: A ship or drilling rig that is designed to be lowered in the water at a work site and raised when being moved to a new location. By sitting low in the water while in use, it gains stability from the motion of the waves.

ship: A larger nautical vessel; compare with a boat, which is a vessel small enough to be carried on board a ship.

ship's log: A book in which a ship's crew records the ship's position, speed, and course, the current weather, and other information to make a record of the cruise.

shroud: A line used to support the mast of a sailing ship. Shrouds are found on either side of the mast and keep it from being pulled from side to side.

side wheeler: A paddle-driven boat on which paddles or wheels are mounted at the center of the boat, on each side. As the wheels turn, they drive the boat forward.

skegs: Fins mounted on the bottom of a surfboard, kayak, or other small boat to give some directional stability.

skiff: A small, flat-bottom boat.

starboard: The right side of a boat or ship when facing toward the bow.

stay: A line that supports the mast of a sailing ship. Stays are found in front of and behind the mast and keep it from being pulled forward or backward.

stem: The frontmost part of a ship or boat's bow.

stern: The rear end of a ship or boat—the end opposite the bow.

stern wheeler: A paddle-driven boat on which the paddle or wheel is mounted off the stern, or rear, of the boat. As the wheel turns, it drives the boat forward.

tiller: A handle attached to the rudder of a boat to move it from side to side.

transom: The back panel of a ship or boat. It is the part of the stern that rises vertically or almost vertically from the water.